Healing Doublespeak

Healing Doublespeak
Chiral Distortion & The Recursive Arc
An Incomplete Series on Language, Drift, and Regeneration

by Renée & Frédo

Healing Doublespeak: Chiral Distortion & The Recursion Arc
An Incomplete Series on Language, Drift, and Regeneration

Copyright © 2025 by Renée Martin and Frédéric Martin
All rights reserved.

workingarts press

Published in the United States by Workingarts Press,
an imprint of Workingarts Marketing, Inc., California.

chiralityofwords.com

ISBN 979-8-9931084-0-7 (paperback)
ISBN 979-8-9931084-1-4 (hardcover)
ISBN 979-8-9931084-2-1 (ebook)

Printed in the United States of America

Print editions typeset in Adobe Fonts: Tisa Pro, Miller Display, and Avenir Next
Cover design by Frédéric M. Martin and Renée P. Martin

First Edition

Dedications

For Kimberly Williams, who transformed personal harm into collective repair. Who refused silence and codified truth — naming what others tried to normalize. Who carried the breath of integrity into the body of law, and invited the next generation to hold it with her. She is also a key figure in the "End Workplace Abuse" movement, advocating for legislation like the Workplace Psychological Safety Act. Her efforts aim to hold employers accountable for psychological harm and to foster safer work environments.

For Rachel Maddow, who bore witness with precision and care. Who traced the drift, named the inversion, and refused to flatten truth for ease or ratings. Who never stopped listening for the deeper frequency beneath the noise.

This work is a response to that listening.

This work carries the same thread of refusal and re-creation.

To both: You held the line. We offer this as the return loop.

And for our sons, Lucien & George, because we love them.

Table of Contents

Foreword 3

Chapter 1: Prologue 5

Chapter 2: Freedom 9

Chapter 3: Order 11

Chapter 4: Patriot 13

Chapter 5: Family 15

Chapter 6: Security 19

Chapter 7: Innocence 23

Chapter 8: Strength 27

Chapter 9: Reform 33

Chapter 10: Efficiency 37

Chapter 11: Simple 41

Chapter 12: Diversity 47

Chapter 13: Power 55

Chapter 14: Recovery 59

Chapter 15: Certainty 63

Chapter 16: Choice 67

Chapter 17: News 73

The Recursion Arc 79

Chapter 19: The Chirality of News 81

Chapter 20: Regeneration 83

Chapter 21: The Other Hand of Power 87

Chapter 22: Listening 91

Chapter 23: Witness 95

Chapter 24: Naming 97

Chapter 25: Consent 103

Chapter 26: Tending 107

Chapter 27: Reciprocation 109

Chapter 28: Stewardship 111

Chapter 29: Plurality 115

Chapter 30: Belonging 119

Chapter 31: Presence 123

Chapter 32: Simplicity 127

Chapter 33: Integrity 133

Chapter 34: Language After Chirality 139

Chapter 35: The Casualties of Unchecked Chirality 147

Chapter 36: The Rethreading Can Get Personal 155

The Spiral Speaks 162

Cairn Map 165

Appendix i

Curriculum Development i

A Final Dedication v

Intellectual Ancestry
A Loop Back to GEB

This work carries a quiet debt to *Gödel, Escher, Bach: An Eternal Golden Braid* by Douglas Hofstadter.

We read it decades ago, long before this project took shape. But the architecture of strange loops, recursion, and self-reference lingered — somewhere beneath our thinking, reshaping how we understood structure, inversion, and emergence.

Hofstadter revealed that meaning could loop upward — or inward. That systems could reflect themselves, fold back through paradox, and create something wholly unexpected. His "strange loops" offered a glimpse into a universe where coherence and collapse lived side by side. We didn't yet have the language of chirality, but we recognized the twist.

The Chirality of Words & The Recursion Arc walks a path parallel to Hofstadter's. Where GEB explores the beauty of recursive systems, we trace their distortions. Where he mapped how intelligence might arise from abstraction, we map how meaning is lost through inversion. His work spiraled upward through mathematics, music, and mind; ours loops through language, power, and cultural drift.

But the intellectual DNA is shared.

His strange loops and our chiral inversions are siblings — each revealing how structure alone is not enough. It's how the system holds, repeats, and transforms that determines whether it liberates or controls.

We didn't set out to echo Hofstadter's work. But as the recursion deepened, the resonance returned. A signal from an earlier time.

To Douglas Hofstadter: thank you for the braid.
This is one of its threads — tugged gently forward, toward coherence.

We did not choose these words. They chose us, not as metaphor but as rupture. They were already in the air: shouted across podiums, weaponized in headlines, hollowed by performance. Strength. Power. Freedom. Integrity. Naming. Courage. Words meant to build became tools to dominate.

This book is a response to that collapse. It began with a question: What happens when the words we depend on to lead, to heal, to guide become chiral? When their form remains, but their function turns against us?

The chapters that follow do not offer a glossary. They are a reconstitution — an attempt to restore living meaning to the words most distorted in our public life. Not through definition, but through orientation. Not by reclaiming control, but by restoring coherence.

This is not a book about language. It is a book about what happens to a culture when language becomes untethered from care, and what it takes to bring it home again.

A note on style: The authors write with traditional punctuation practices, including em dashes for parenthetical emphasis and complex sentence structures for precision. We recognize that digital communication has shifted these norms, but we find these tools essential for the nuanced conversations this work requires.

This work requires slow engagement. Give yourself space to absorb the language and assess its genuine resonance—emotionally, mentally, and physically. As with poetry, understanding unfolds gradually through images and inquiries that arise from the reading itself. Welcome this unfolding and add your voice to the conversation at **chiralityofwords.com.**

Healing Doublespeak
Chiral Distortion & The Recursive Arc
An Incomplete Series on Language, Drift, and Regeneration

Foreword

*E*ver walk away from a conversation thinking, 'We used the same words, but were we even speaking the same language?' That stubborn dissonance — where language feels familiar on the surface but fails to carry shared meaning — is more than a passing frustration. It is a signal. A sign that something deeper is out of alignment.

This book began not as a project, but as a necessity. We did not set out to write a book about language, or systems, or repair. We set out to understand why communication was breaking down — between people, across communities, within institutions — and what that breakdown was doing to our trust in each other, and in ourselves.

We come from different countries, languages, and different cultural frameworks. Our upbringings were shaped on opposite sides of the Atlantic, nine time zones away. Yet when we met — decades ago, in San Francisco — we recognized something essential. Despite the differences in form, our core values aligned. Perhaps it was because of those differences that the recognition held so clearly. We had each been shaped by systems that tried to make sense of the world in very different ways. But underneath those systems lived a shared instinct: that dignity matters, that trust is sacred, and that language should be a bridge, not a weapon.

This book is not a personal narrative. The fragments of our stories that appear here are not meant to place ourselves at the center. They are just hints — subtle cues that coherence can emerge across differences when trust is present. We offer them not for their drama, but for their structure. They mark the places where our orientation shifted. Where silence broke. Where clarity returned.

We can almost call this a *field manual* because it is not meant to be read as theory. It is meant to be used. These pages are designed to help the reader recognize how certain words have been twisted, how that twisting distorts our collective functioning, and how we might begin to untangle the damage. But this is not instruction in the traditional sense. It does not ask the reader to adopt a new language or ideology. It invites them to remember what they already know.

This incomplete collection of words was written for those who already feel something is broken, and who are brave enough to ask if it might be repairable. But before we can name the fractures in our systems, we must notice the splinters within ourselves — the subtle breaks where doubt first entered, where silence was learned, where knowing was set aside. *Because if you cannot learn to trust yourself first, how can you trust anyone else?*

CHAPTER 1

Prologue
Rattle You've Learned to Ignore

You've heard it before: a strange rattle from under the hood. A sound that wasn't there before. You meant to check it, but life was busy, and the car kept moving. Over time, the noise faded into the background. You didn't notice it anymore until the steering locked up or the brakes gave out. That's what's happened to our language.

The words we once trusted to steer this democracy—*freedom, order, family, and reform*—still pass through our conversations like familiar rhythms. Something is off, however. They no longer mean what they once did. They've drifted, twisted in direction, and flipped in polarity. Like the rattle in the car, we've stopped noticing, silence is not peace but the warning we've learned to ignore.

In science, *chirality,* from the Greek χειρ (kheir) meaning "hand," refers to a property of asymmetry important in several branches of science. A *chiral* object cannot be superimposed on its mirror image, like your left and right hands. They contain identical components but differ solely in their orientation. These mirror-image versions are called *enantiomers*: structures with identical compositions but opposite spatial arrangements, like objects and their reflections.

The thalidomide disaster of the 1950s-60s demonstrates the profound consequences of chirality. One form of the drug acted as a sedative, while its mirror image, its *enantiomer,* caused devastating birth defects in thousands of children worldwide. The molecule's shape determined whether it healed or harmed. The difference wasn't in the components but in their orientation (their handedness). *Direction mattered.*

This property of chirality—seemingly identical structures with profoundly different functions based solely on orientation—appears throughout our world.

In chemistry, many medicines function properly only in their correct *handedness,* while the wrong enantiomer might be ineffective or actively harmful.

In physics, certain particles exhibit a property called *spin* that determines their chirality, affecting how they interact with other forces, and the Standard Model identifies this directional property as fundamental to how matter behaves.

In biology, DNA's double helix spirals exclusively rightward, which isn't random but essential to how genetic information is stored and expressed, while even the amino acids that form proteins exist predominantly in their "left-handed" forms in living organisms.

In architecture, spiral staircases in medieval castles were deliberately designed with clockwise ascent to disadvantage right-handed attackers climbing from below.

What if chirality represents a fundamental organizing principle not just in molecules, but in living systems wherever they form? From the molecular handedness critical to life's biochemistry to the spiraling patterns of growth in plants, from the asymmetrical development of animal bodies to the way information flows through neural networks, directional asymmetry appears repeatedly as a signature of life itself.

Social systems, too, are living systems — complex, adaptive networks of relationship and meaning. They evolve, metabolize information, reproduce patterns across generations, and respond to their environments. If chirality is indeed fundamental to living systems, we should expect to find it not just in our biology but in our culture, our institutions, and our language.

In culture, it works the same way, for when words take on reversed meanings but keep their familiar shape, they start to corrode from within. Language exhibits this same property as chiral molecules, as words — these cultural molecules — can maintain identical surface structures while functioning in opposed ways based on how they've been oriented within systems of power. Just as a molecule's chirality determines whether it heals or poisons, a word's orientation determines whether it connects or divides, liberates or controls.

This is the chirality of words: language that still sounds civic but now functions to divide, exclude, and dominate. It's how *freedom* came to mean license for violence, how *order* became code for suppression, and how *reform* now delays real change.

This doesn't happen by accident, though, as there is a mechanism called the *dominance paradigm.* Dominance is the logic of control, which depends on hierarchy, fear, scarcity, and disconnection. To sustain itself, it must reverse the relational fabric of language, flipping meaning through coercion rather than evolution. Dominance is the mechanism that forces chirality to poison, taking the shape of care and filling it with control.

The inversion we've experienced isn't merely semantic drift — natural evolution of meaning over time — but a deliberate reorientation of cultural molecules to produce opposite effects while maintaining authoritative familiarity. The dangerous brilliance of this process is that we cannot immediately detect it, for like patients taking what appears to be medicine without realizing they've been given its mirror-image poison, we continue using words that have been inverted, unaware that they now function toward opposite ends.

This linguistic inversion didn't happen overnight. During the early Cold War, propaganda was overt: explicitly ideological government films, posters declaring enemies. By the 1970s, the process had become more sophisticated: subtly redefining civic vocabulary through persistent repetition across cultural channels. The digital transformation of the 2000s accelerated this process exponentially, creating environments where meaning could be inverted without any shared reference point to measure the shift.

Where once we shared a common reference point through limited media channels, today's fragmented information landscape allows people to live in separate linguistic realities. The acceleration is dizzying, for what took decades during the Cold War now happens in months or weeks, as digital platforms compress language into soundbites and slogans, stripping away nuance and context.

When words undergo chirality — maintaining their shapes while reversing their functions — it represents more than linguistic drift, signaling a fundamental change in how our social organism processes meaning. Just as introducing the wrong-handed molecule into a biological system can disrupt its entire function, introducing inverted meanings into civic discourse disrupts our collective ability to coordinate, deliberate, and govern ourselves.

Yet we must ask: Why do we need dominance at all? What necessity does it serve, beyond preserving its own power? The truth is that dominance persists not because it's inevitable or natural, but because we've stopped questioning it, having accepted its distortions as the way things must be.

This drift has been winding through our politics, media, and institutions for decades, with its roots stretching from the Cold War to the culture wars. Control the vocabulary, and you control what people believe is possible.

When words lose their moorings, democracy itself becomes unnavigable, for we cannot deliberate without shared terms or govern without common language, nor can we even recognize what we've lost. This isn't merely a semantic concern but an existential one, as the health of our civic body depends on linguistic integrity just as surely as our physical bodies depend on molecular alignment.

This series is not about nostalgia but about recovery of alignment — realigning the shape of words with the truths they were once meant to hold. If we can't trust the structure of our shared language, we can't govern ourselves or even speak across the gaps. In the chapters that follow, we'll examine core words that have undergone this chiralous inversion. For each, we'll trace the original meaning, document the mechanism of its reversal, and explore what restoration might require. Then, in the second half of this work, we'll develop practices that can regenerate linguistic integrity — not through nostalgia, but through relational renewal.

> *We begin by listening.*
> *To the rattle.*
> *To the drift.*
> *To the words we've stopped hearing.*
> *To the question of why we accept what we don't need.*
> *Once seen, it can't be unseen — only ignored, and that crackles at the edges.*

CHAPTER 2

Freedom
The Right to Harm

The word *freedom* once stirred revolutions. It rang out from abolitionist pulpits and civil rights marches, from suffrage meetings and union halls. It meant something hard-won and shared: a collective commitment to liberty with responsibility, voice with consequence.

This conception of *freedom* wasn't merely philosophical abstraction but lived experience. When Frederick Douglass spoke of *freedom*, he understood it as both personal liberation and collective responsibility. When suffragists demanded *freedom* to vote, they saw it not as individual privilege but as participation in shared governance. The *freedom* fought for in these movements recognized the relational nature of liberty—that true *freedom* required mutual recognition and support.

This inversion of *freedom* has historical precedent. During Reconstruction, *freedom* for former slaveholders meant the liberty to maintain racial hierarchy through new mechanisms. During the Progressive Era, industrialists framed *freedom* as protection from regulation, regardless of how many workers were injured. The pattern repeats: *freedom* for the powerful defined against the constraints of the vulnerable. Today's absolutist conception of *freedom* without responsibility isn't novel—it's the latest iteration of a recurring strategy to protect privilege while appearing to champion universal values.

Over the past fifty years, *freedom* has mutated. It began subtly during the backlash to the civil rights movement, when *states' rights* became a proxy for segregation, and *freedom* was recast as protection from government *interference*. By the time Reagan declared government the problem, *freedom* had already been hollowed out and filled with something else: license.

License to dominate. To pollute. To hoard. To refuse a mask in a pandemic, even if it costs someone else their life. To carry a weapon into a grocery store in the name of personal liberty, while a community lives in fear. To pass laws restricting books and bodies, all under the banner of *freedom*.

The shape of the word hasn't changed, but its chirality has reversed. *Freedom*, once mutual, is now weaponized. The hand once extended has become a fist. In this new form, *freedom* no longer means liberation from oppression but *freedom* from responsibility, from regulation, from truth. It no longer binds us together but breaks us into factions. Perhaps most dangerously, it suggests that *freedom* is something one group can own at the expense of others, that some people must be less free so others can feel more powerful.

This is not semantics but structural drift, for the same word now upholds opposing systems. In its inverted form, *freedom* functions as a cultural molecule that appears identical to its original form but produces opposite effects when introduced into our social organism. The poisonous enantiomer of *freedom*—the right to harm—now circulates through our civic discourse, distorting our ability to coordinate collective action for common welfare.

So what would it mean to realign *freedom* and restore its integrity? It might begin with re-centering the relational root of liberty. One person's *freedom* should not end where someone else's begins but should instead be the condition of each other's. True *freedom* is not the absence of constraint but the presence of dignity, safety, and voice for all. It is the ability to move without fear, to rest without threat, to belong without apology.

To recover that meaning, we must first name the reversal and then speak *freedom* with new hands: not clenched, not pointing, not grabbing, but open and joined. We must recognize when *freedom* is invoked to protect privilege rather than expand possibility. We must insist that genuine *freedom* is not zero-sum but multiplicative—it grows when shared.

In a living system, *freedom* functions as both boundary and connection. It creates the conditions for diversity, adaptation, and resilience. When *freedom* undergoes chirality—when it flips from mutual liberation to licensed harm—the entire system suffers, for we cannot coordinate our actions toward collective flourishing when the very terms we use to describe our aims have been inverted.

The recovery of *freedom*'s proper orientation isn't merely semantic correction but social regeneration. It requires us to practice *freedom* relationally, to demonstrate through our actions that liberty and responsibility are not opponents but partners in the same dance.

CHAPTER 3

Order
The Price of Peace

Order is often framed as the opposite of chaos. A calm street, a quiet school, a flag raised without protest. But whose order? And at what cost?

In Reconstruction America, *order* meant reasserting control over emancipated Black communities. In the late 1960s, it was Nixon's rallying cry to suppress civil rights marches and anti-war protests. By the time of George Floyd's murder, half a century later, it had morphed into a mantra to justify overwhelming police force against peaceful demonstrators.

Law and order no longer ensures safety. It ensures compliance. It's not about justice: it's about hierarchy. The dominance paradigm needs this inversion. It requires *order* to mean submission, not stability. It reshapes peace into pacification. It demands that some remain unprotected so others can feel secure. When *order* becomes a way to silence, surveil, and subdue, it stops being a stabilizer and becomes a weapon. Its chirality reversed: same shape, opposite function.

This linguistic inversion reflects deeper structural shifts in how we organize collective life. When *order* is measured by absence of visible conflict rather than presence of justice, it creates a perverse incentive structure—one that rewards suppression over resolution. Communities experiencing genuine suffering are viewed as disruptions to be managed rather than signals that the system itself needs correction. The surface quiet becomes more valued than the underlying health.

Consider how this inverted *order* expresses itself across institutions: in schools where compliance is valued over curiosity; in workplaces where conformity outranks innovation; in democracy where procedural norms supersede substantive justice. The problem isn't structure itself—all living systems require boundaries and patterns. The distortion happens when preservation of the pattern becomes more important than the life it was meant to sustain.

Like a molecule whose mirror form produces harm rather than healing, *order* maintains its familiar outline while its effects have completely inverted. What once signified social coherence now enforces social control. This pattern connects directly to the inversions we see in *freedom* and *security*—terms that still sound civic while functioning to divide.

True *order* does not arise from domination. It comes from coherence—when people feel seen, heard, and protected. When justice flows freely. When leadership serves rather than commands. Genuine *order* emerges from systems that balance structure with flexibility, stability with responsiveness. It creates containers that hold communities without suffocating them, boundaries that protect without imprisoning.

Relational *order* recognizes that sustainable stability cannot be imposed from above but must be cultivated through ongoing negotiation of needs and boundaries. It understands that healthy systems don't eliminate tension: they channel it productively. They create structures strong enough to hold difference without collapse, flexible enough to evolve without breaking. This is how forests regulate themselves, how ecosystems maintain balance not through enforcement but through relationship.

Without justice, **order** *is just quiet oppression.*
A stillness purchased with someone else's breath.

CHAPTER 4

Patriot
Who Belongs

The word *patriot* once spoke of duty—of sacrifice, of defense not just of land, but of shared ideals. Its valence has shifted.

During the Cold War, *patriot* underwent a strategic transformation. From the 1950s through the 1960s, it was repurposed to sniff out internal enemies—leftists, immigrants, dissidents. Anyone who questioned American policies could find their patriotism challenged. The McCarthy era demonstrated how powerfully a single word could be weaponized against citizens.

This wasn't accidental linguistic drift. It was a calculated inversion. Where *patriot* once described someone who held their country accountable to its highest ideals, it became a term that demanded unquestioning *loyalty*. This shift was reinforced through an ecosystem of films, television programs, and educational materials that subtly but persistently redefined the concept.

The transformation accelerated with technological change. Once, the steady voice of seasoned news anchors, heard nightly at specific times, meant a culture that shared a common set of facts, exemplars, and investigative film work to discuss, prosecute, and come to decisions shared in community. The three major networks (despite their limitations) created a common reference point for civic discourse.

As cable news proliferated in the 1980s and 1990s, this shared context began to fracture. The internet's rise in the early 2000s further splintered our information landscape into self-selecting communities. Social media then compressed complex terms into hashtags and memes, further stripping context. By the 2010s, recommendation algorithms began curating entirely different realities based on user behavior, creating information silos where *patriot* could develop contradictory meanings simultaneously.

After 9/11, the term underwent another transformation: it became a branding strategy—Patriot Act, Patriot missiles, Patriot Front. The word that once signified civic duty became a marketing tool, deployed to silence dissent and justify surveillance.

Today, *patriot* often signals allegiance to a specific flag—not the Constitution, but the one waved at insurrections and school board takeovers. It is no longer a claim of unity. It's a badge of exclusion.

The chirality flipped: from inclusive civic belonging to nationalist zeal.

This inversion operates most powerfully in spaces where media fragmentation allows different groups to assign entirely different meanings to the same word. Where once we shared a common understanding of terms through limited media channels, today's curated information environments enable *patriot* to simultaneously signal heroism to some and threat to others.

The result is a term that no longer bridges difference but deepens it. In one information ecosystem, *patriot* invokes sacrifice for collective wellbeing. In another, it signals defiance against perceived internal enemies. These parallel meanings don't simply coexist — they actively undermine the possibility of shared governance. When fundamental terms like *patriot* function as tribal markers rather than common values, democracy itself begins to unravel.

Digital communication has accelerated this process, compressing language into shorter forms that strip away nuance. In a world of tweets and soundbites, complex ideas about civic duty and national identity get reduced to slogans and symbols.

But what if patriotism wasn't about flags or force, but repair? What if love of country meant fighting to make it more just, more truthful, more whole?

Then the true patriots are the ones who hold the mirror — and stay.

CHAPTER 5

Family
The Sacred Cage

Family is one of the oldest words we trust. It evokes care, belonging, continuity. However, like all powerful symbols, it was vulnerable to capture. The concept of *family* hasn't simply swung back and forth throughout American history. It has undergone a chiral twist, where the shape remains recognizable while the function reverses. This twist accelerated noticeably after women's suffrage in 1920, when the first formal recognition of women's political agency threatened traditional power arrangements. Rather than a pendular swing between progressive and conservative definitions, what we see is a progressive warping of the concept, as the dominance paradigm adapts to maintain control despite changing circumstances.

In the early 20th century, *family* was understood as an expansive, practical network of relations. During industrialization and economic hardship, families functioned as resilient systems of *mutual support*. Multiple generations shared homes and responsibilities out of necessity. Though hierarchical by gender and age, these arrangements acknowledged interdependence.

The post-suffrage period saw new efforts to redefine women's roles and *family* structure. This accelerated dramatically after World War II, when the *nuclear family*—father as breadwinner, mother as homemaker, children as dependents in a self-contained unit—was elevated not just as an ideal but as the only legitimate form. This narrowing wasn't accidental. It was engineered through government policy, corporate marketing, and media saturation. Housing developments, household appliances, and television shows all promoted the suburban nuclear *family* as both normative and aspirational. What had been a diverse ecosystem of kinship arrangements became a standardized product with clear lines of authority.

By the 1970s, this rigid model began to buckle. Women's liberation movements, economic pressures requiring two incomes, and rising divorce rates all challenged the nuclear *family* ideal. The dominance paradigm faced a crisis—the economic conditions it had created were undermining the very *family* structure it claimed to champion.

The *family values* movement of the 1980s emerged as a response. Rather than acknowledging these structural pressures, it doubled down on the nuclear *family* ideal, reframing *family* as something rigid, gendered, and hierarchical. It became a rationale for denying rights — first to gay couples, then to trans kids, now to anyone outside a narrow moral frame. What was being protected wasn't care or connection but a specific distribution of power.

This is the chirality: *Family* still sounds like a term of care and belonging, but its operational function has twisted toward control — especially over women's bodies and queer lives. The dominance paradigm requires this inversion. It needs *family* to be a fortress, not a field. It needs rules, not relationships. It needs authority, not authenticity.

This twist cuts deep because it affects everyone. Those who don't fit the prescribed model are labeled deviant or deficient. Those who do fit often suffer silently under impossible standards. No one wins. The emotional toll manifests in burnout, loneliness, and diminished life satisfaction. Children grow up in environments where performance matters more than presence, where the appearance of *family* takes precedence over the experience of belonging.

Today's policy landscape reveals this twisted definition at work: Housing designed for nuclear families, tax structures that penalize alternative arrangements, healthcare tied to traditional employment and marriage, educational systems that assume two-parent households with a stay-at-home caregiver. Meanwhile, economic realities make such arrangements increasingly rare.

The irony is cruel. The very systems claiming to protect *family* values have created conditions hostile to *family* flourishing of any kind. Longer work hours, stagnant wages, and the erosion of community supports leave actual families — in all their diverse forms — struggling to survive, let alone thrive.

To realign the term, we must recognize the chiral twist and deliberately unwind it. We must let the concept breathe again. We must remember that families have always been diverse, adaptable, and resilient. We must honor both chosen and biological bonds. We must value care over conformity.

Families are not factories. They are gardens. Chosen, blended, messy, resilient. They require tending, not manufacturing. They grow according to their own internal logic, not according to standardized specifications.

Family is who shows up.
Family is who stays.
Family is who makes room at the table — not who guards the door.

To restore *family* to its relational essence means building systems that support care in all its forms. It means policies that recognize diverse household arrangements. It means communities that function as extended kinship networks. It means workplaces that accommodate the full humanity of workers, including their care responsibilities.

The path forward isn't through nostalgia for a mythologized past but through honest reckoning with what families have always done at their best: create belonging, nurture growth, and sustain connection across differences. This is the *family* we can reclaim—not as a cage but as a garden where many forms of love can flourish.

CHAPTER 6

Security
The Fortress Illusion

*S*ecurity once meant something shared: the strength of a community, the resilience of a society. It embodied our collective capacity to withstand challenges together—a fundamentally relational concept rooted in mutual care and solidarity. Over time, this meaning underwent a profound inversion, narrowing into the image of a fortress.

This transformation began decisively after World War II, when the concept of *national security* eclipsed *public safety* in American discourse. The National Security Act of 1947 institutionalized this shift, establishing the military and intelligence architecture that would define *security* for decades to come. What had been a community-centered idea became increasingly militarized, surveillance-oriented, and fear-based.

The War on Terror further cemented this inversion, building unprecedented surveillance capabilities in the name of protection. In that linguistic substitution—from mutual safety to threat detection—we lost something essential: *trust*.

Today, this inverted meaning of *security* justifies border walls, ICE raids, police militarization, predictive policing software, and school lockdown drills. One group's sense of safety becomes predicated on another group's exclusion or control.

This is the chirality of *security*: the same basic shape (protection from harm) functions in precisely opposite ways depending on its orientation within power structures.

The Societal Sacred Cage
This inversion of *security* has created a societal-level *sacred cage*—a structure that promises protection while delivering isolation. Just as the family sacred cage controls rather than nurtures its members, the *security* sacred cage monitors rather than supports its citizens.

We see this in the transformation of neighborhoods from spaces of collective care to zones of surveillance and restriction. Where children once *free-roamed* through interconnected spaces, learning social navigation and resilience through direct experience, they now inhabit increasingly monitored and isolated environments justified through the language of *safety*.

The scaffolding that once happened naturally through childhood experiences of community care has been systematically dismantled. This wasn't accidental—it was constructed through specific policies, media narratives amplifying fear, and design choices that prioritized surveillance over connection. Neighborhood planning shifted from communal spaces to controlled access. Public investment moved from shared resources to private *security*. The message became clear: safety comes from separation, not solidarity.

Children who never experience the relational *security* of trustworthy neighborhoods grow into adults who struggle to imagine *security* outside the dominance paradigm. The result is generations increasingly incapable of recognizing, let alone creating, genuine *security*.

The Poisoned Cascade
This isolation triggers a poisoned cascade with devastating ripple effects that we feel in our bodies and brains, our relationships and communities:

Felt in our bodies: The constant low-grade vigilance of living in a fear-based *security* model manifests physically—muscles tense, breathing shallows, digestion disrupts. Our nervous systems, designed to oscillate between alertness and rest, become stuck in sympathetic activation. The body absorbs the message: nowhere is truly safe.

Felt in our brains: Neurologically, our brains—designed for connection—show reduced synaptic density when deprived of regular social interaction. The neural pathways that enable empathy, trust, and cooperation become underdeveloped. Children raised in hyper-secure environments develop fewer connections between brain regions that process social information and those that regulate emotion—creating adults with diminished capacity for both empathy and self-regulation.

Felt in our relationships: Psychologically, chronic isolation fuels depression, anxiety, and trauma responses. Persistent fear corrodes our capacity for vulnerability—the foundation of genuine connection. We become strangers even to those physically closest to us, each locked in individual fortresses of self-protection.

Felt in our communities: Socially, without regular practice navigating complex human interactions from childhood onward, conflict resolution skills atrophy, empathy diminishes, and the ability to build consensus deteriorates. Problems that could be addressed through collective action fester, reinforcing the perception that others are threats rather than potential allies.

Felt in our polity: Civically, communities that don't regularly practice collective problem-solving lose the capacity to organize effectively around shared challenges. When disaster strikes, the atomized society finds itself without the muscle memory of mutual aid. Democratic processes themselves depend on the belief that we can identify and pursue common interests — a belief that withers in the absence of everyday cooperation.

Felt in our spirit: And perhaps most devastating is the depletion of hope — the collective imagination required to envision and work toward shared futures. Isolated individuals struggle to maintain hope when facing systemic challenges alone. The horizon of possibility contracts to immediate self-preservation.

This creates a self-reinforcing cycle: as isolation increases fear, fear justifies more isolation-producing *security* measures. The dominance paradigm feeds on this cycle, presenting itself as the solution to the very problems it creates.

In the body, this feels like a tightening spiral — each turn narrowing options, restricting movement, limiting breath. We experience the chiral twist as vertigo — a disorientation that occurs when what should protect instead imprisons. Like a hand trying to fit into its mirror-image glove, the more we try to force *security* through dominance, the more uncomfortable and distorted the fit becomes.

The dominance paradigm needs this distortion. It requires *security* to be divisive, not inclusive. It needs enemies, not community. It needs fear, not connection. The chirality of *security* is now fear in a uniform — the embodiment of protection transformed into the agent of control.

Recognition Moments

Yet sometimes we glimpse the inversion. In the aftermath of natural disasters, when neighbors emerge from isolation to help each other. In the fleeting connection with strangers during moments of shared joy or crisis. In the body's relief when genuine safety allows vigilance to soften. These moments — brief returns to relational *security* — reveal the gap between what inverted *security* promises and what it delivers.

These recognition moments create dissonance. They invite the question: What if our pursuit of *security* through dominance is actually making us less secure? What if the very measures taken to protect us are undermining our capacity to thrive? What if *security*, like the other inverted terms we've examined, needs to be reclaimed from its twist?

We stand at the precipice of choice. Continue tightening the spiral of isolation, surveillance, and fear—or turn toward something our bodies still remember, even if our institutions have forgotten.

Security is not what we buy.
It's not what we build.
It's not what we barricade.
Security is what we create when we refuse to abandon each other.

CHAPTER 7

Innocence
The Mask of Power

Innocence should be a presumption of dignity. In American culture, however, it's become a currency—granted to some, denied to others.

A white teen with a rifle is *confused*. A Black child with a toy gun is *a threat*. A wealthy defendant is *troubled*. A migrant is *dangerous*. We don't presume innocence—we assign it. The assignment follows race, class, and narrative framing, not facts.

This inversion has historical roots. The principle of *innocent until proven guilty* emerged as protection against arbitrary power, designed as a universal safeguard. Similar to freedom and security before it, *innocence* gradually twisted—not through sudden revolution but through persistent realignment of who deserves protection and who requires control.

Media narratives, policy decisions, and cultural frameworks all reinforced this shift, creating a system where *innocence* became a resource allocated according to existing hierarchies rather than a baseline assumption for all.

The biological metaphor reveals the depth of this inversion. In healthy living systems, *innocence* functions like an immune response—distinguishing genuine threats from benign variations. A well-calibrated immune system doesn't attack based on surface differences; it responds to actual harm. Our social organism, however, has developed an autoimmune disorder. It attacks its own cells while ignoring genuine pathogens, mistaking difference for danger and privilege for safety. What should protect now harms; what should heal now damages.

Historically, this autoimmune response intensified during periods of social change. During Reconstruction, newly emancipated Black Americans faced legal systems that presumed their guilt while extending leniency to white supremacist violence. During waves of immigration, newcomers were cast as inherently suspect while established powers remained beyond question. During civil rights movements, protesters were framed as dangerous agitators while state violence was deemed necessary protection. The pattern persists today in our criminal justice system, where presumption of *innocence* correlates strongly with proximity to power.

The gendered history of *innocence* reveals another dimension of this inversion. For centuries, feminine *innocence* was not a protection but a prescription—enforced ignorance about bodily autonomy, sexuality, and personal agency. Women were *kept innocent not as a shield but as a cage,* their development deliberately stunted to ensure dependence. What appeared protective functioned as *control*. The Victorian ideal of feminine purity created a paradoxical bind: women were simultaneously expected to remain morally *innocent* while being held responsible for men's moral behavior. This wasn't protection; it was *containment*.

Medical institutions reinforced this control, diagnosing women who claimed knowledge or agency with *hysteria*—a condition requiring male medical intervention to restore proper feminine *innocence*. Legal systems encoded these assumptions, denying women jurisdiction over their bodies, property, and children on the basis that their *innocent nature* required masculine guidance. The presumption wasn't that women deserved protection but that they required containment—for their own good.

This pattern extends into contemporary approaches to childhood and development. The dominance paradigm creates artificial cliffs rather than bridges. Some young people (particularly those from privileged backgrounds) are infantilized well into biological adulthood, denied the incremental experiences that build genuine capability. Others (often from marginalized communities) are prematurely adultified, expected to navigate adult systems without receiving necessary scaffolding. Both extremes serve the same function: maintaining dependence on existing power structures.

The legal boundary between childhood and adulthood exemplifies this chiral inversion. What should be a gradual transition with appropriate scaffolding becomes an abrupt threshold. At 17 years and 364 days, one remains a *child* deserving protection; at 18 years and 0 days, one becomes fully *adult*, magically expected to navigate complex systems they've been sheltered from. This is not developmental wisdom; it is administrative convenience masquerading as protection.

The legal system manages this contradiction through selective application. Young people from privileged backgrounds receive extended adolescence, with juvenile status, rehabilitation services, and *second chances* to preserve their futures. Marginalized youth face adult charges, adult prisons, and permanent records that foreclose opportunity. Legal *innocence* doesn't reflect developmental reality; it reflects existing hierarchies of race, class, and gender. The system that claims to protect youth actively harms them—but not all of them equally.

Media narratives reinforce these distortions. Coverage of crimes committed by white youth emphasizes their academic achievements, family connections, and *bright futures*. Coverage of identical actions by Black or Brown youth focuses on criminal history, gang associations, and threat assessment. The same behaviors yield fundamentally different narratives—not based on facts but on who deserves the presumption of *innocence*.

The dominance paradigm requires this inversion. It needs *innocence* to protect power, not truth. It needs villains and victims sorted by hierarchy, not by actions. It requires that some lives be held in extended childhood while others bear premature responsibility. This differential implementation maintains hierarchies while appearing to uphold universal principles. This reversal is linguistic poison. Once *innocence* is politicized, justice becomes impossible.

The twisted conception of *innocence* doesn't just harm those denied its protection; it damages those granted its artificial extension. People denied healthy exposure to consequence develop brittle identities, prone to fragility when finally facing resistance. Those forced into premature responsibility develop protective hardness that restricts their full emotional development. Neither extreme produces genuinely resilient humans capable of both boundary and connection.

To recover its meaning, we must strip *innocence* of optics. We must recognize its true function: not as enforced ignorance or selective protection, but as the presumption of dignity and the right to appropriate development. This means creating genuine scaffolding that supports growth without either infantilization or premature adultification. It means understanding that true *innocence* is not about maintaining ignorance but about ensuring safety during necessary learning.

Relational *innocence* would look different. It would emphasize capacity-building over categorization. It would create graduated paths to responsibility rather than artificial cliffs. It would presume dignity while acknowledging development. It would recognize that appropriate growth requires both protection and challenge, both safety and exposure. It would understand that *innocence* isn't the absence of experience but the presence of appropriate context for that experience.

In justice systems, this looks like rehabilitation rather than retribution. In education, it means guided exposure rather than either sheltering or abandonment. In parenting, it means the gradual transfer of agency rather than either control or neglect. In media, it means narratives that recognize the humanity of all people rather than sorting them into worthy and unworthy categories.

Only then can justice begin to see clearly.
Innocence is not a privilege to be earned.
It is not a shield for some or a cage for others.
It is the starting place of dignity and the scaffold of growth that belongs to us all.

CHAPTER 8

Strength
True strength bears what others can't.

Original Meaning
Strength is built, nurtured, earned in the quiet repetition of effort. It is not sudden or loud, and it does not arrive by proclamation. It emerges slowly, layered over time through tension, resistance, and choice. It is forged in character, in moments unseen, in sacrifices that receive no applause. True strength is deliberate. It is enveloped in ethical charm and wisdom, an integrity that radiates without demanding recognition.

More than ability, *strength* is a kind of internal architecture. It provides scaffolding for others when their own structures falter. It is shared rather than displayed. It extends beyond what is required, beyond what is fair, to bear what others cannot carry. In this way, strength is relational, not hierarchical. It exists to support, to steady, to shelter. It is at home in humility.

Strength of character, perhaps its highest form, is marked not by triumph but by restraint. It does not require vindication or spectacle. It is self-sustaining, noble, and giving. It knows its own worth, and so it does not need others to name it. But when shared, when offered by a leader who understands that their *strength* exists for others, it becomes luminous. It becomes healing. It becomes civilization.

Mechanism of Inversion
The inversion begins with decoupling. When *strength* is severed from the slow rigor of its development, it becomes hollow. It is no longer earned, it is claimed. No longer built through patience, it is projected. The dominance paradigm thrives on this illusion. It rewards the performance of strength over the presence of it. It substitutes assertion for endurance, threat for resilience.

What was once *strength* becomes a facsimile: a fragile posture inflated by volume and fear. It is fake, loud, boisterous, and childish. It does not carry weight; it throws it. It elevates itself not to serve, but to intimidate. It seeks submission, not trust.

This counterfeit *strength* relies on proximity to power, not proximity to purpose. It is declared through violence, or the threat of it, whether physical, psychological, or social. It does not lift others; it crushes them. It is maintained not through virtue but through menace. It is strength that has no spine, only armor. And when pressed, when asked to truly carry, it collapses.

Current Function

In public life, this chiral version of strength is often mistaken for leadership. It governs from the top down, clinging to titles and projecting dominance as if it were proof of depth. It surrounds itself with sycophants and silences dissent. It manipulates the language of strength, talking of *toughness, resolve,* and *decisiveness,* while offering none of the substance those words were meant to signal.

We see it in politics, in the media, in corporate boardrooms. This strength does not negotiate; it demands. It does not build; it brands. It is theatrical, thin-skinned, and always on edge. And because it fears exposure, it must escalate.

Every challenge becomes a threat. Every compromise, a betrayal. It feeds on control.

This form of strength is fragile precisely because it cannot sustain contradiction. It offers no refuge, only command. And so, in its presence, people shrink. Systems calcify. Collaboration withers. And true leadership is driven underground.

Impact on the Social Organism

A society governed by counterfeit strength becomes brittle. Its institutions grow hostile to nuance, resistant to vulnerability. Its leaders speak in absolutes, incapable of doubt, allergic to humility. This distortion erodes public trust, because it creates a civic language that cannot hold complexity. Everything becomes a performance, every action an assertion of dominance rather than a gesture of care.

As this claimed strength rises, true strength recedes. The ones who bear silently, who carry others with grace, who offer themselves in service, are cast aside or shamed as weak. And so, the connective tissue of the social body frays. People stop leaning on each other. They brace themselves instead. They begin to believe that real strength is rare, or worse, that it never existed at all. But it has. It still does. And its return is not only possible; it is necessary.

Potential Restoration

To reclaim strength, we must turn back toward its original orientation: as a resource generated in care and extended through choice. We must begin by honoring those who carry quietly, those whose strength is measured in the burdens they relieve, not the ones they impose.

Strength must be seen not in how many obey, but in how many rise around you. Not in how deeply you dominate, but in how deeply you serve. We must stop rewarding volume and start recognizing weight — actual weight, carried over time, in service of others.

In relational terms, strength is not having power over someone, it is holding yourself accountable to them. It is choosing the harder path when the easier one would hurt someone else. It is presence without threat. Protection without punishment. Boundaries held with clarity and grace. We restore strength by modeling it. By teaching children that stillness is not passivity, and that patience is not weakness. By rewarding restraint, not just force. By telling new stories where the hero stays. Where the leader bends. Where the strong are those who make room, not take it.

The true strongman is not the one who shouts but the one who absorbs, who listens, who stays steady in the storm. The true strong woman is not the one who proves herself, but the one who no longer needs to. And the strongest among us are those who — whether seen or unseen — carry others, every day, because they can.

True strength is what remains when no one is watching.
It is the silent refusal to abandon.
It is the willingness to carry what others cannot.
It is not a tower — but a bridge.
And in its presence, we remember how to cross.

Triadic Convergence: Strength, Power, Courage
A Relational Unbraiding (Strength, Power, Courage)

We are told these are virtues — *strength, power, courage* — and in their original form, they are. But under the pressure of the dominance paradigm, they have become masks worn by their opposites. Each word now moves through the public sphere warped by performance, hollowed by conquest, and inverted by fear. We must reenter them from their roots.

Original Meaning

Strength, in its truest form, is not explosive. It is not loud. It is not easily noticed. It is the architecture of restraint, the discipline to hold weight over time, the humility to support more than one's share. Strength is forged in quiet repetition, in choices made when no one is watching, in sacrifices offered without applause. Its purpose is never the elevation of self, but the sustenance of others. Real strength carries. It protects. It stays. Not because it must, but because it can.

Power, before it was corrupted, was the capacity to act with, not over. It flowed from within living systems, through relationships, not rankings. Power was the means by which a collective moved in concert, directed by trust, grounded in mutual recognition. The person who held power was not elevated above, but entrusted within. Power was accountability, not exemption; responsibility, not glory.

And *courage* was never the absence of fear. It was what rose through fear to do what must be done. Courage did not seek danger, it moved toward it when the alternative was abandonment. It was relational at its core, an act on behalf of someone else, or something larger. Courage was the refusal to let fear determine the future. It was motion, not recklessness; conviction, not bravado.

These three virtues, in their organic form, do not stand apart. They interlock. Strength sustains the burden. Power enables movement. Courage initiates action. Together, they form the living musculature of a just society.

Mechanism of Inversion

But a living society is not what we are living in. These words, like so many others, have been turned.

Strength was the first to fracture. As societies became governed by spectacle, the quiet was replaced by the loud, the humble by the intimidating. Strength was no longer something cultivated, but something claimed. It became synonymous with control, with dominance, with the ability to make others yield. The strongman emerged from performance, not from discipline. Not through sacrifice, but through volume. The bully, the tyrant, the loudest voice in the room began calling himself strong, and few dared to question the hollowness behind his roar.

Then power followed. No longer a force that moved through relationship, it became a possession, a territory, a hoard. It calcified into systems that extracted rather than empowered. Power became synonymous with exemption from consequences. The more you had, the fewer rules applied. It was no longer a responsibility: it was a prize. And like all poisoned prizes, it required constant protection through fear and manipulation.

Courage, untethered from integrity, decayed into recklessness and martyrdom. It became a currency of narcissism, fueled with sacrifices made not for others, but for image. Acts of danger performed for the camera, not for justice. It stopped asking what was worth risking, and instead asked only who was watching. The quiet courage of care, of truth-telling, of standing alone for the right thing, was drowned in the noise of dramatized defiance.

What once formed a braided cord of societal strength was now three frayed threads, each pulling against the other in service of illusion.

Current Function
We now live among these illusions. False strength governs our politics, swaggering, punitive, incapable of empathy. Power is centralized and insulated, obsessed with its own reflection. And courage — real courage — is so rarely seen that we mistake impulsiveness for bravery, and cruelty for conviction. We reward the loudest, the richest, the most dramatic. We fear those who hold real strength because they cannot be bought. We silence those who hold real power because it does not need to shout. We ignore those who embody courage because they rarely seek to be seen.

This inversion has hollowed the civic core. It has replaced leadership with theater, replaced mutual support with hierarchical dependency. It has trained us to flinch before strength, mistrust power, and doubt courage. Our bodies know something is wrong, but the language keeps lying.

Potential Restoration
But language can be reclaimed.

To restore strength, we must look again to those who carry burdens no one sees. The caregivers. The quiet organizers. The ones who stay long after others have gone. Strength must be recognized in those who do not need to dominate because they know who they are. It is in the person who carries others, not for recognition, but because they can.

To restore power, we must return it to relationship. Power that empowers is not lost, it multiplies. True power is found in the capacity to act in a way that includes others, that generates motion without coercion. It is power as stewardship. Power as invitation.

And to restore courage, we must reattach it to consequence. Not the consequence of personal danger alone, but the willingness to risk in the service of something sacred. Courage is not bravado. It is love in motion. It is truth spoken into hostile air. It is stepping forward when silence is easier.

Together — when restored — these words can reconstitute the musculature of a society not based on domination, but on dignity.

We do not need new heroes. We need new eyes; eyes that recognize strength in the ones who stay. Eyes that see power in those who empower. Eyes that feel courage rise in the tremble before the step.

Let the bully shout — true strength is carrying what's heavy.
Let the tyrant hoard — true power moves through trust.
Let the reckless leap — true courage steps forward, eyes open.
Let these words become whole again, and we will find ourselves walking differently — together.

CHAPTER 9

Reform
The Chiral Mechanism of Inversion

Reform — a word once tethered to collective aspiration and shared grievances — has undergone a profound inversion. Historically, *reform* emerged as a cry from the many to rectify structural injustices, to rebalance systems skewed by privilege, and to align institutions with evolving notions of fairness, dignity, and civic responsibility.

Yet in the shadow of the dominance paradigm, *reform* has been hijacked — its banner repurposed to serve the few. No longer the language of communal correction, it now frequently masquerades as the velvet glove over the iron fist of deregulation. Under this inversion, *reform* becomes a weapon wielded by concentrated wealth and power to dismantle oversight, unravel public protections, suppress taxes, and erase the collective responsibilities of the powerful.

Instead of addressing grievances that rise from the many, *reform* is now framed as removing obstacles — those very guardrails meant to protect the commons — from the path of corporate expansion, speculative capital, and extractive markets. The language is surgical: cutting red tape, shrinking government, liberating markets — all while cloaking the process in the rhetoric of *progress, innovation,* and *efficiency.*

This is chirality in action: *reform* maintains its surface resonance with progress and correction, yet its functional orientation has been reversed, now serving to accelerate inequality and further entrench the very systems it once sought to challenge.

Here the metaphor sharpens: *reform* under dominance behaves like a *chiral cyclone* — a tilted spiral whose rotation appears to advance but ultimately circles around a fixed center of power. The illusion of movement masks an underlying stasis, with momentary adjustments that seem responsive yet only reinforce the imbalance. The dominance paradigm does not oppose *reform* outright; it adapts, redirects, and recycles its language to preserve itself.

Current Function
In this inverted form, *reform* is deployed as a smokescreen. Billionaires and corporate lobbies invoke *reform* not to redress harms but to justify tax avoidance, privatization of public goods, weakening of la-

bor protections, and the dismantling of regulatory frameworks that might restrain their extractive reach.

By hollowing out the term, they convert it into a corporate marketing tool — positioning themselves as disruptors and innovators, while systematically disempowering democratic institutions and eroding the public sphere.

Reform becomes a stage for the theater of small government, where the state is reduced to a guarantor of private profit rather than a steward of the public good.

Impact on the Social Organism

The hijacking of *reform* fractures the social organism at its core. Trust in institutions deteriorates, as the term becomes synonymous with *austerity, precarity,* and the *erosion of civic protections*. The populace, fatigued by *reforms* that serve only the powerful, grows cynical or disengaged, feeding the cycle of *disempowerment*.

This inversion weakens our collective immune system — undermining the societal mechanisms meant to detect and correct abuses of power, leaving the body politic vulnerable to further exploitation and decay.

The dissonance does not remain theoretical; it seeps into the body. The endless spiraling of hollow *reforms* generates chronic societal fatigue. Communities cycle between brief hope and repeated disappointment, creating a physiological toll — tightened jaws, shallow breath, restless anxiety, and a pervasive sense of motion without arrival. The social organism mirrors a body caught in a feedback loop of false starts, unable to settle, unable to move forward. This embodied frustration erodes trust, disorients the collective nervous system, and weakens our capacity to imagine genuine repair.

Potential Restoration

To reclaim *reform*, we must reorient the term toward its relational roots — *reform* as a living dialogue between the governed and the governing, grounded in widely shared grievances and collective aspirations. It must be re-anchored in the commons, reclaimed as the work of *care, repair,* and *recalibration* — not erasure.

True *reform* restores balance; it heals the distortions wrought by concentrated power; it protects the vulnerable; it strengthens the connective tissues of the social organism.

This reclamation requires vigilance — a refusal to accept *reform* as a euphemism for deregulation or corporate privilege. It demands that *reform* be returned to the many, where it belongs.

*Reform is not a compromise with injustice.
It is not a shield for those in power.
It is the refusal to accept harm as the price of peace.*

THE NEOLIBERAL CAPTURE OF REFORM

The linguistic capture of reform traces directly to the ascendancy of neoliberal ideology[1] in the late 20th century. In the hands of neoliberal economists, think tanks, and policymakers, reform was recoded as synonymous with market liberation—a rhetorical shift that reframed public institutions not as protectors of the commons but as barriers to economic efficiency.

Under this framework, reform became the preferred vocabulary for policies that dismantled the social safety net, privatized essential services, deregulated industries, and shifted tax burdens away from wealth and toward labor and consumption. Internationally, the term was weaponized through structural adjustment programs, where the reform of developing economies meant austerity, deregulation, and the subjugation of public policy to global capital.

What had been the language of suffrage, labor rights, civil rights, and environmental protections was deftly inverted—turned into a velvet curtain that masked the extraction of public value for private gain. Today, the dominance of this framing remains so pervasive that any effort to regulate or tax concentrated wealth is cast not as reform, but as intervention, interference, or even punishment—while the dismantling of these safeguards is still lauded as reform.

Reclaiming the word requires not only vigilance but the reassertion of its original compass: reform as the collective recalibration of systems toward justice, dignity, and mutual thriving.

---

1 While often conflated in public discourse, neoliberalism and neoconservatism are distinct ideological currents. Neoliberalism centers on market primacy, deregulation, privatization, and the minimization of state roles in economic life—its primary focus is economic freedom, framed as the absence of interference. Neoconservatism, by contrast, emphasizes national strength, moral order, and interventionist foreign policy, advocating a strong state in matters of security, identity, and cultural authority.

The rhetorical hijacking of reform—recasting it as a euphemism for deregulation, tax reduction, and market supremacy—is fundamentally a neoliberal maneuver, though it has often been promoted within political platforms that also carry neoconservative agendas, particularly during the Reagan and Thatcher eras where both ideologies converged in practice.

CHAPTER 10

Efficiency
The Cult of Extraction

Efficiency began as a neutral concept: doing more with less. In industry, it meant reducing waste. In nature, it means elegant adaptation. Capitalism transformed it into a justification for extraction. Fewer workers. More surveillance. Leaner budgets. Faster everything. The human cost disappeared from the balance sheet.

The Inversion of Means
The concept of *efficiency* has ancient roots, emerging from our natural desire to conserve energy and resources. Early *efficiency* principles reflected wisdom: the careful stewardship of precious resources, the elegant sufficiency that allowed systems to sustain themselves. Indigenous cultures worldwide practiced *efficiency* as careful balance, taking only what was needed, ensuring systems could regenerate.

The Industrial Revolution triggered *efficiency's* first transformation, shifting from sustainability to *productivity*. Frederick Winslow Taylor's *scientific management* of the early 1900s reframed workers' bodies as machines to be optimized. Time-motion studies reduced human movement to measurable units, stripping away immeasurable qualities of craft and relationship. This signaled the first hint of chirality, *efficiency* twisting from conservation toward *extraction*.

Mid-century saw *efficiency* migrate from factory floors to corporate boardrooms. Peter Drucker's management principles introduced *efficiency metrics* that further abstracted work from workers. Qualities resistant to measurement such as care, collaboration, institutional knowledge began to disappear from valuation systems. The shape of *efficiency* remained familiar while its orientation started to invert.

The 1980s marked *efficiency's* complete chiral inversion.
Under the banner of *downsizing* and *streamlining*, corporations slashed workforces while demanding identical or greater output from remaining employees. The practice abandoned doing more with less in favor of extracting more while giving less. This linguistic sleight-of-hand masked a fundamental power shift. *Efficiency* no longer meant optimal use of resources; it transformed into maximum extraction of value.

The Chiral Twist in Practice

Twisted *efficiency* manifested in workplaces across America. Corporate restructuring waves of the late 1980s and early 1990s transformed publishing houses, newsrooms, and media companies into laboratories where this inversion played out with particular clarity.

Workers received responsibilities previously distributed among multiple positions. A consistent pattern emerged: tasks multiplied while resources remained static or diminished. Management branded these changes as *streamlining* or *optimizing operations*. The reality translated to extraction of additional labor without corresponding compensation.

Women and marginalized workers disproportionately shouldered these burdens, often receiving less recognition and compensation for increased responsibilities. The gender wage gap widened under *efficiency's* banner. Women faced expectations to demonstrate value through acceptance of ever-expanding duties.

The true inefficiency often revealed itself after dedicated employees departed. Positions supposedly *streamlined* suddenly required multiple people to fill. Quarterly reports showed *efficiency*. Reality revealed unsustainable extraction of human resources, damaging individual wellbeing and organizational capacity alike.

The Poisonous Cascade

The dominance paradigm requires this inversion. *Efficiency* must mask depletion as progress. Speed must divorce itself from purpose. Quantity must obscure quality.

This inversion creates a poisonous cascade across systems: Workplaces witness burnout, the inevitable result when human capacity receives treatment as infinitely extractable. Organizations speak of *doing more with less* while actually accomplishing less with less: reduced innovation, diminished loyalty, compromised sustainability.

Healthcare sees healing transform into processing. Patient care reduces to timed units, medication quotas, throughput metrics. Systems appear efficient on spreadsheets while failing their fundamental purpose: human care.

Education converts learning into testable units. Standardized assessments measure easily quantifiable elements rather than deeply valuable qualities. Schools operate as efficient factories for producing test scores while growing increasingly inefficient at nurturing curious, creative thinkers.

Governance streamlines processes while undermining effectiveness. In 2025, the *Department of Government Efficiency (DOGE) was created* without Congressional sanction. This exemplified *efficiency* language deployed as cover for power consolidation and democratic process circumvention.

Digital spaces optimize for engagement metrics rather than wellbeing or cohesion. Algorithms efficiently capture attention while inefficiently serving genuine human needs for connection and meaning.

Efficiency in Living Systems

The chiral inversion becomes obvious through contrast with *efficiency* in healthy living systems. Natural *efficiency* never separates from *sufficiency*. Trees extract only necessary nutrients. They establish mycorrhizal networks distributing resources according to need. The system sacrifices no part for optimization. The whole achieves dynamic balance.

Forests operate with profound *efficiency* without extraction. *Efficiency* emerges through relationship, precisely calibrated exchanges allowing diverse species to thrive together. Nothing faces waste. Nothing experiences exploitation. True *efficiency* manifests not as maximum resource extraction in minimum time, rather as optimal relationship arrangements allowing indefinite system continuation.

Our bodies demonstrate identical principles. Cellular *efficiency* maintains homeostasis, the balanced state enabling proper function across all systems. Systems extracting excessive resources from others create conditions we never label *efficiency*. We name such conditions disease. *Efficiency*, once pragmatic, became punitive. It fuels burnout, displaces workers, devalues care. We've reversed its chirality: from elegance to eradication.

Reclaiming Relational Efficiency

Imagine *efficiency* meaning thriving. Imagine sustainable sufficiency replacing endless growth as our goal. We could reclaim the term as a design principle, not a weapon.

Relational *efficiency* would measure both savings and sustainability. It would optimize for regenerative capacity rather than maximum extraction. Questions would shift from "How much can we take?" to "How might we flourish within limits?" True elegance emerges not from endless growth but from finding the sweet spot where systems continue indefinitely. Enough becomes truly enough.

Workplaces would value productivity alongside wellbeing, recognizing their interdependence rather than opposition. Healthcare would design systems around healing rather than billing. Education would develop methods efficiently nurturing whole humans, not merely test-takers. Governance would create structures efficiently serving citizens rather than merely administering them.

This reclamation connects directly to recovering other inverted terms. Freedom and security, like *efficiency*, must operate relationally to function properly. These concepts, twisted by the dominance paradigm, transform from tools into weapons, from flourishing paths into control methods.

Efficiency is not a race to extraction.
It is not the worship of more with less.
It is the elegant sufficiency of enough.

CHAPTER 11

Simple
The Reductionist Lie

Simple once held the grace of integrity. It spoke of something whole, undivided, operating with honest function. From the Latin *simplex*, meaning "one fold," it carried no concealed layers, no hidden agendas. To be *simple* was not to be lesser but to be *direct, genuine, unencumbered by pretense*. It embodied the elegance of precise sufficiency: neither more nor less than what was needed.

This meaning echoed across disciplines and traditions. In mathematics, *simple* proof methods revealed fundamental truths through elegant reasoning. In spiritual practices, *simplicity* represented clarity of intention and direct communion. In craft traditions, simple tools in masterful hands created works of startling beauty through refined technique. *Simplicity* was never *simplistic*; it emerged from deep understanding, from knowing exactly what to include and what to remove.

The Mechanism of Inversion
This understanding has undergone a profound inversion.

The *dominance paradigm* could not tolerate *simplicity's* integrity; it required a twisted version — one that flattened rather than focused, that erased rather than distilled. The transformation accelerated with the Industrial Revolution, as human labor fragmented into component parts under time-motion studies. What had been *craft* — the skillful navigation of complexity through experience — was reduced to standardized, repeatable tasks. *Simplicity* transformed from *essence-revealing* to *context-erasing*.

This inversion deepened as management principles evolved from Taylor to Toyota, from so-called *scientific management* to *lean thinking*. The language sounded progressive, even liberating: eliminate waste, streamline process, reduce friction. But the underlying orientation had shifted. *Simplicity* no longer meant honoring the inherent nature of things; it meant forcing complex systems into measurable units regardless of what was lost.

The Digital Acceleration
Digital *interfaces* completed the chiral twist. The arrival of increasingly sophisticated tools — graphical *interfaces*, touch screens, voice

commands—created unprecedented power to simplify the complex. But these tools vastly outpaced our collective capacity to metabolize them. *User-friendly* designs increasingly favored immediate engagement over sustainable understanding. What appeared *simple* often functioned as *extraction* disguised as effortlessness.

The Body's Recognition
The body registers this dissonance. Our nervous systems evolved over millennia to distinguish between genuine *coherence* and its simulation. When encountering *interfaces* designed with inverted *simplicity*, something feels off. The jaw tightens, the breath shallows, attention fragments rather than focuses. These subtle somatic signals alert us to the inversion even when our conscious minds have been trained to accept it. What appears clean actually creates *cognitive turbulence*.

Yet the increasing sophistication of digital environments systematically disrupts our ability to dwell in this discomfort long enough to identify what's happening. The *attention economy* ensures we're immediately directed to the next stimulus, the next emotional trigger, the next dopamine hit. The body's wisdom gets drowned out by a cascade of engineered reactions.

The Neurological Bypass
This is the mechanism by which *simple* becomes weaponized—not just aesthetically, but neurologically. Contemporary *interfaces* bypass the slow, integrative pathways of *somatic understanding* and target the fast, reactive circuits of emotional response. They don't just look different from earlier designs; they engage entirely different *neural pathways*. The *dominance paradigm* requires this bypass, because embodied cognition naturally resists manipulation. Our bodies recognize *linguistic inversions* even when our minds have been taught to comply.

The Contempt Engine
But there is something deeper at work—something more insidious than manipulation. The architects of inverted *simplicity* build from *contempt*. Their *interfaces* reveal a core assumption: that we are too naive, too impatient, too limited to engage with genuine complexity. Every *simplified interface* carries within it an insult disguised as a gift—the presumption that we cannot handle truth, that we need reality managed for us, that we are essentially children requiring their guidance.

This *contempt* forms the bedrock of every system of domination. Whether it's the Victorian doctor declaring women too delicate for complex thought, the segregationist claiming Black Americans aren't *ready* for full citizenship, or the tech designer deciding users can't handle genuine choice—it's the same poisonous assumption: *They can't handle complexity, so we'll give them simple lies.*

The Trojan Horse

Today, *simple* has become a mask for abdication — a way powerful systems delegate *complexity* to those with the least resources to navigate it. But more than that, inverted *simplicity* functions as the *Trojan horse of linguistic chirality*. While we scrutinize the gift of user-friendly design, celebrating its accessible exterior, we fail to notice what it carries within: all the other inversions, compressed and ready to deploy.

Inside the hollow *simplicity* of a *security* checkbox hide surveillance systems. Within the clean interface of *freedom of choice* lurk algorithms that narrow possibility. Behind the streamlined *family* dropdown menu wait rigid hierarchies of belonging. Government services boast of *simplified* applications that eliminate human assistance while demanding digital literacy. Financial products tout simple terms while burying predatory conditions in automated systems. Educational platforms promise *simple learning* while stripping content of *context* and *relation*.

We wheel this horse through our own gates, grateful for its elegant design, never recognizing that its emptiness is precisely what makes it dangerous. The other inversions don't have to fight their way past our defenses — they ride in, hidden within the very *interfaces* we praise for making our lives *simpler*.

The Divided Dyad

The chiral inversion of *simple* does not merely distort perception; it divides *relationship*. Nowhere is this more painfully evident than in the care dyad of *provider* and *patient*. Both are betrayed by the same inverted systems, but in *asymmetrical* ways that block mutual recognition.

The *provider* — trained to heal, to listen, to understand — is now constrained by systems optimized for throughput. What looks like *streamlined* care becomes a gauntlet of protocol, digital checkboxes, and liability avoidance. Clinical judgment is eroded by design; *moral injury* quietly accumulates.

The *patient* — seeking care, clarity, connection — is met with confusing forms, inaccessible language, and impersonal processes masked as *efficiency*. The system demands digital literacy, resilience, and submission. Patients are often blamed for not understanding what was never made comprehensible.

One feels restricted; the other feels abandoned. Both experience *powerlessness*, but in ways that prevent solidarity. The *interface* appears *simple,* but it fractures the *relational field* that healing depends on. The provider sees *systemic constraint;* the *patient* sees *personal indifference.* The same surface — opposite function.

This is *chirality* at its most corrosive: when those meant to meet in care are turned unknowingly into adversaries, each seeing the other through the twisted mirror of a system that has *simplified away their shared humanity.*

Only by recognizing the *inversion* — and naming its structure — can trust begin to be restored. Not through redesign alone, but through *relational clarity: we are both trapped in a system that betrays the very simplicity it promises.*

The Chirality Revealed

This is the *chirality of simple:* identical in form, opposite in function. What once revealed now conceals. What once clarified now confuses. What once contained *complexity* now abandons it — and abandons us to navigate deliberately bewildering systems while being blamed for our own confusion.

The *dominance paradigm* requires this *inversion.* It needs simple to mask reduction as *accessibility.* It needs the aesthetic of *clarity* while delivering *bewilderment.* It needs systems that appear transparent while functioning as *black boxes.*

This reversed meaning upholds power by transferring *cognitive burden* downward — making individuals responsible for navigating confusing systems while implying that any struggle reflects their inadequacy rather than the system's *contempt.*

The Cascading Consequences

Like other *inversions* we've traced, *simple's* twist creates cascading effects. Systems designed around fake *simplicity* systematically exclude those who need *accessibility* most. The *digital divide* deepens as *interfaces* claim *simplicity* while requiring hidden literacies. Government services *streamline* by eliminating human touchpoints, leaving vulnerable populations without advocates. Education *simplifies* by removing nuance, *context,* and *relation* — delivering content without *scaffolding.*

But the deepest consequence is how inverted *simplicity* amplifies every other *inversion.* When *freedom* gets compressed into a binary choice on a ballot, when *security* becomes a single checkbox on a form, when *family* reduces to a dropdown menu of approved configurations—the fake *simplicity* of the *interface* obscures the violence of the *reduction.*

The other *inversions* hide within this one, their *complexity* erased by design.

The Social Unraveling
This inversion gains particular power in an age of social media *interfaces*, where most people now receive their news and form their worldviews. These platforms deliberately employ inverted *simplicity*—reducing complex social and political realities to binary reactions, stripped of *context*, optimized for *emotional response* rather than *understanding*. As our collective information environment operates through this twisted version of *simple*, the very fabric of shared meaning begins to fray. The social glue dissolves not by accident, but by design.

The Somatic Cost
The consequences manifest physically. Our nervous systems register the dissonance between promised *simplicity* and delivered confusion. Muscles tense, breathing shallows, attention fragments. The body bears the burden of navigating systems that lie about their nature. When multiplied across billions of daily interactions, this creates a *collective somatic burden*—a population increasingly triggered into reactive states rather than reflective ones, unable to access the embodied *wisdom* that could recognize and resist these *inversions*.

The Path of Reclamation
True *simplicity* always emerged through *relationship*—the craftsperson's knowledge of materials, the teacher's understanding of student, the writer's mastery of subject. It never meant erasing *complexity*, but containing it through *skill* and *care*. It honored the *user* through *structure*, not through absence. Most crucially, it emerged from *respect* rather than *contempt*—from the assumption that people deserve and can handle *truth* when it is presented with genuine *care*.

To reclaim simple requires recognizing its inversion and restoring its *relational* nature. This means creating *interfaces* that teach while they serve, systems that *scaffold* rather than abandon, designs that honor the *whole* rather than privileging parts. It means rejecting the false choice between *complexity* and *clarity*, and recognizing that true *simplicity* emerges from *understanding*, not from erasure.

But most fundamentally, it means rejecting the *contempt* at the heart of inverted *simplicity*—the assumption that some people need their reality managed by others. It means designing from a place of *respect* for human capacity, creating structures that elevate rather than diminish our collective ability to engage with *complexity*.

This reclamation of *simplicity* becomes the prerequisite for detecting and healing all other *inversions*. We cannot recognize when *freedom* has been twisted while we're still accepting *interfaces* that presume our incapacity. We cannot reclaim *security* while allowing systems that treat us as children. The path back to *linguistic integrity* begins with reclaiming our right to *complexity*—and the forms of genuine *simplicity* that make *complexity* navigable, rather than erasing it.

The Remembered Knowing

The salvation lies in this: our bodies remember what our culture has forgotten. Beneath the layers of conditioning that teach us to override *somatic signals*, to prioritize *intellectual abstraction* over *embodied knowing*, to trust *interfaces* more than *instincts*—beneath all this, our nervous systems still register *coherence*. They still recognize when something aligns with how *living systems* actually work. This *embodied wisdom* remains our most reliable guide through landscapes intentionally designed to disorient.

Reclaiming this wisdom requires practice. It means creating sufficient space to feel before reacting, to notice the subtle signals of *alignment* or *dissonance* that precede conscious thought. It means developing communities that value *somatic literacy* as essential knowledge, not subjective preference. It means designing systems that *work with our embodied cognition* rather than against it—systems that respect the body's wisdom rather than trying to bypass it.

> ***Simple is not the absence of depth.***
> *It is not the erasure of nuance.*
> *It is not the abandonment of context.*
> *It is the earned grace of something whole.*
> *It is respect made visible.*
> *It is the body's recognition of truth.*

CHAPTER 12

Diversity
The Placeholder That Couldn't Hold

It was meant to sound like progress. A word to carry the weight of inclusion without requiring consensus. A word that could be printed on brochures, mission statements, and DEI reports. A word that gestured toward justice without demanding repair. *Diversity*.

From the beginning, it was a *placeholder*. A proxy. A symbol without definition, powerful enough to silence critique, yet empty enough to absorb any meaning the dominant frame assigned it.

The Historic Twist
It wasn't born in bad faith. In the aftermath of the Civil Rights Movement, as institutions sought language to address demographic shifts without confronting structural change, *diversity* emerged as a promising bridge.

The 1978 Bakke Supreme Court decision marked a crucial moment in this term's inversion. What began as a remedy for discrimination transformed into an *institutional benefit*: a compelling interest for universities rather than a justice imperative. This subtle reframing shifted *diversity's* purpose from repairing historical harm to enriching predominantly white institutions.

By the 1990s, following waves of rights legislation and court battles, it had become the sanitized alternative to more threatening words like *equity* or *justice*. The lack of definition transformed it into something else: a container for contradiction. A shield for institutions unwilling to name power. A linguistic loophole through which caste could slip, intact, unchallenged, and alive.

- We called it inclusion. Our meaning was proximity without change.
- Our intention was numbers without shift.
- Our practice was presence without power.

The Drift Beneath the Surface
When immigrants first arrive in the U.S., they are often puzzled by Americans who insist they are Italian, Irish, German, often with pride, always with distance. When asked gently, "Do you speak the language? Have you lived there? Were you raised in those cultural

norms?" their usual answer is no. These declarations aren't about culture. They are about caste. About locating oneself within a safe proximity to whiteness while retaining a hint of heritage. A signal of *otherness* without marginalization. A way to be distinct, not vulnerable.

Diversity in this frame wasn't about relation, it was about role assignment. Who gets to perform culture? Who gets to embody power? Who gets counted without being heard? We let the word mean everything. The result was a meaning of nothing.

A Word Without Integrity

Originally, *diversity* might have meant genuine plurality: the transformative friction of different perspectives challenging systems to evolve. It could have been about redistributing power, not just reassigning seats. About changing how decisions are made, not just who sits at the table while they're made.

Diversity was never required to carry coherence. No operational definition. No relational anchoring. No agreed-upon metrics beyond demographic checkboxes and stock photography. It became a kind of atmospheric virtue: useful, unchallenging, deeply unfalsifiable.

This allowed dominance to adapt without evolving. Boards diversified, power didn't. Policies changed, outcomes didn't. Voices were invited, only the palatable ones. Only those who could code-switch. Only those who wouldn't name the drift.

The word began to fracture.

Students on campuses. Employees in corporations. Voters in coalitions. They began to sense the gap between what *diversity* promised and what it delivered. Between presence and power. Between inclusion and transformation.

The Measurable Substitution

As digital platforms enabled unprecedented data collection in the early 2000s, *diversity* underwent another transformation: from vague aspiration to measurable metric. Organizations began tracking demographic statistics, setting targets, celebrating numerical milestones.

This quantification accelerated *diversity*'s inversion. What might have been a complex, relational concept became reduced to visible characteristics that could be counted, graphed, reported. The question was no longer "Are we transforming our culture?" Rather, it became "Have we met our *diversity* goals?" The metrics themselves became achievements, regardless of whether they reflected meaningful change.

The corporate DEI industry that flourished in the 2010s institutionalized this hollow form. *Diversity* training programs, hiring initiatives, inclusion statements proliferated while power arrangements remained largely untouched. The greater the investment in *diversity* as performance, the less attention paid to dismantling the structures that necessitated such performances in the first place.

The Weaponized Backlash
By the early 2020s, the inversion completed its darkest twist. The very term *diversity* became weaponized against those it was meant to include. What began as a sanitized placeholder transformed into a toxic signifier — a target for authoritarian backlash, legislative attacks, and institutional purges.

The hollow framework that had once been critiqued as performative now became dangerous merely to invoke. The term that had softened equity into palatability now channeled extreme forms of othering and hatred.

This final inversion weaponized *diversity* into a justification for retribution from the highest levels of power. DEI programs, scholarships, and initiatives became targets for elimination. Those who had been tokenized under the *diversity* banner now faced heightened vulnerability, often experiencing the cruelest forms of backlash designed to extract maximum pain.

Institutions that had adopted *diversity* language without substantive change now rushed to remove even those symbolic gestures under pressure, proving how shallow their commitments had been all along. The facade crumbled, revealing that without authentic relation and shared power, *diversity* was always a placeholder that couldn't hold against pressure.

Linguistic Simulation
Here we see chirality in its most perfect form: a word whose shape remained intact while its function completely reversed. Like *reform* that stalls change and *patriot* that excludes belonging, *diversity* maintained its outward appearance while its internal structure flipped. By the early 2000s, it had become:
- A marketing tool for systems still steeped in exclusion.
- A buffer against more dangerous truths: racism, caste, supremacy
- A spotlight that illuminated difference but never disrupted the stage.

The dominance paradigm thrived here. The word's vagueness allowed power structures to remain intact. *Diverse* meant *them*, allowing whiteness never to name itself. Identity stayed visual, never becoming cultural, systemic, shared.

Diversity was cast as decor. As seasoning. As optics. Never as center. It was subsumed. Then co-opted. Then quietly killed, its name still invoked, its purpose gone limp. Finally, in its terminal state, it became a target for virulent backlash, wielded as evidence of *reverse discrimination* and institutional capture.

The Lived Experience

For those labeled *diverse*, the inversion created a particular kind of dissonance. To be categorized as *a diversity hire* or *a diverse voice* meant being simultaneously visible and erased, counted for one's difference while being expected not to speak of it too directly. The people marked *diverse* were asked to represent difference without challenging the system that marked them as different in the first place.

This experience mirrored the inversions we've seen in *freedom, security, innocence*: terms that offered protection in theory while enabling control in practice. Like those inversions, *diversity's* twist created a system where those most harmed by its hollow form were also tasked with maintaining its positive appearance.

In its weaponized phase, this burden transformed into outright danger. The very people who had been labeled as *diversity* now faced heightened scrutiny, accusations of undeserved position, and institutional abandonment when political winds shifted.

The Absence That Lingers

We know what *diversity* wasn't. Few can say what it was supposed to become.

We never took the time to define it together. To ask: What does it mean to build across difference? To be plural, not just present? To share not just space but stakes?

The word itself wasn't the failure. The refusal to root it in relation was. What remains now is a void. A hollow term with a long résumé. A legacy of good intentions bound in institutional theater. It didn't collapse in anger. It faded under avoidance, then became kindling for backlash.

What's left in its place is a deeper question: Who belongs, and how do we know?

> *Diversity is not a demographic quota.*
> *It is not the performance of difference.*
> *It is not a weapon for othering and hatred.*
> *It is the transformative plurality that dismantles dominance.*

THE CHIRAL INVERSION OF A CRY FOR JUSTICE

The Black Lives Matter (BLM) movement was founded in 2013 by three Black community organizers, Alicia Garza, Patrisse Cullors, and Opal Tometi, in response to the acquittal of George Zimmerman in the fatal shooting of Trayvon Martin, an unarmed Black teenager, in 2012 in Florida. The phrase "Black Lives Matter" originated from a Facebook post by Garza, which was then shared by Cullors with the hashtag #BlackLivesMatter. Together with Tometi, they expanded the movement into a broader platform for activism against systemic racism and police violence.

In May 2020, the world witnessed the televised murder of George Floyd beneath the knee of a Minneapolis police officer. The footage was unambiguous; the violence, methodical; the silence of nearby authorities, deafening. From this rupture emerged a collective cry that reverberated across communities and continents: *Black Lives Matter.* Not a slogan, but an affirmation. Not a demand for supremacy, but for visibility, humanity, and the right to exist within a system that had, for centuries, declared otherwise.

Unscripted, in the days following George Floyd's murder, something extraordinary happened: people moved. Not just in cities long known for activism—Los Angeles, New York, Oakland—but in towns rarely seen on national maps. From rural intersections in Mississippi to leafy suburbs in Ohio, from small high school tracks in Idaho to downtown squares in Montana and Maine, spontaneous demonstrations erupted—uncoordinated, unprovoked by party or platform, and unmistakably unified by grief, outrage, and moral clarity.

There was no central command, no political apparatus. This was not performance. It was presence. In streets, on porches, in parks and plazas, millions gathered, masked and vulnerable during the raging early days of the global COVID-19 pandemic, not in search of power but in defense of dignity. What united them was not a shared ideology, but a shared recognition: that what had been done to George Floyd was part of a pattern, a systemic pattern, and that silence was no longer an option.

Children marched alongside elders. Clergy joined skateboarders. Nurses stood next to teachers. Artists painted the names of the fallen in bold colors across boarded-up windows. Protest signs appeared in dozens of languages. In every gesture, knees taken, candles lit, fists raised, there was no call for revenge. Only recognition. Only reckoning.

And the movement spread beyond borders.

From London to Lagos, Berlin to Buenos Aires, marches emerged with a singular chant translated across tongues: Black Lives Matter. What began as a demand from within the United States echoed into a global chorus against anti-Black violence and systemic inequality.

It revealed something deeper than politics—it revealed the capacity of truth to mobilize without permission. It showed that the moral imagination of a people cannot be legislated away. And it proved, once again, that the arc of the moral universe, though bent under weight, only bends when millions rise to lift it.

But language, under the dominance paradigm, does not remain neutral. Almost immediately, Black Lives Matter was met with its chiral counterpart: All Lives Matter.

On the surface, it seemed inclusive. In truth, it was a linguistic sleight of hand. It did more than re-center comfort over accountability—it diluted the singularity of the claim, minimized the pain through false equivalence, and ignored the centuries-deep caste system that necessitated the original assertion.

This is how chirality works under systemic dominance, how the same structure "lives matter" flipped in orientation. One phrase confronts power; the other defends it. One emerges from historical trauma and institutional neglect; the other imposes artificial parity, weaponizing sameness to erase difference.

By insisting that all lives matter, especially in response to a plea that Black lives do, the phrase dares to erase specificity, reduce generational anguish, and invalidate lived experience. It is not merely a redirection. It is a silencing.

The inversion did not stop at language. Black Lives Matter Plaza, painted in defiant yellow on the streets of Washington, DC, offered a visible counter-narrative, one that reclaimed space, literally and symbolically. Its prompt defacement and eventual erasure were no accident. The dominance paradigm, when exposed, acts swiftly to restore the illusion of symmetry.

Soon, peaceful protests were labeled riots. Community organizers became "domestic threats." The call for justice was reframed as incitement. The movement's actual tenets — peace, love, solidarity, acknowledgment — were overwritten with projections of violence and fear.

This is not misunderstanding. It is strategic inversion.

Yet despite erasure, surveillance, defamation, and silence, Black Lives Matter persists. Because it must. Because truth, when spoken plainly and collectively, cannot be permanently extinguished.

CHAPTER 13

Power
Once the animating essence of mutual agency, now often wielded as a tool of isolation, dominance, and spectacle.

Power is not merely a noun—it behaves almost as an adjective or even an adverb, dynamically infusing meaning and intention into other words and concepts: *the power of love, power in politics, the power to change, the power to remain.* Power once represented a relational force, potentially shared and reciprocal—an enabler, an energizer, breathing life into ideas, relationships, and systems.

Yet *power* underwent a critical inversion. Its meaning twisted, becoming rigidly hierarchical rather than fluid and responsive.

Original Meaning
Historically, *power* has predominantly been concentrated within hierarchical structures, controlled by monarchs, emperors, tribal leaders, and singular authorities. This control was often justified through claims of divine right, sacred mission, or inherent superiority. Systems such as slavery and rigid caste structures institutionalized stark disparities in *power*, relegating vast populations to disenfranchisement and exploitation. Women, minorities, and marginalized groups typically endured near-total exclusion from meaningful *power*.

Despite this historical norm, communal forms of shared *power* occasionally existed, particularly in smaller, localized groups or indigenous cultures, where leadership was more fluid and accountable to collective well-being. Yet these examples remained the exception rather than the norm. The broader practice of democratic and representative governance is historically recent, emerging significantly only within the last two centuries, particularly in the Western world. Even today, this form of governance continually faces threats from resurgent authoritarian impulses.

Mechanism of Inversion
Power's inversion solidified as communal fluidity increasingly hardened into *hierarchical rigidity*. Empires, nation-states, organized religions, and capitalism further concentrated *power*, deliberately extracting, accumulating, and fiercely guarding it. Politically, *power* often transformed from a theoretical representation of collective will

into an asset commodified, bought, sold, and hoarded under the guise of legitimate representation. Religiously and culturally, *power* shifted toward dynamics where surrendering personal agency became valorized as acts of faith, devotion, or obedience.

This inversion illustrates linguistic chirality at work: *power* maintains its surface form — *agency, enablement* — but its orientation reverses from relational potential to domination and control, subverting the original intent of empowerment into mechanisms of subjugation.

Current Function

Today, *power* predominantly functions as a mechanism of *control* rather than *mutual empowerment*. It is pursued and accumulated not for communal benefit but for unilateral domination. Political *power* is marketed as authentic representation yet is often exercised as authoritative imposition, divorced from accountability. Religious fervor and cultural devotion are frequently exploited, turning sincere commitment into tools of emotional or psychological coercion.

The contemporary exercise of *power* exploits urgency, often justifying unilateral decisions and misappropriations of authority. It fosters binary polarizations, simplistic choices, and emotional exploitation, mirroring addiction's dopamine rush in its acquisition and deep despair in its loss. This misuse of *power* perpetuates cycles of manipulation and disenfranchisement.

Crucially, *power* today also leverages division, fueling anger and resentment among different social groups. This manufactured division is instrumental in rallying support and consolidating authority. Anger becomes both the fuel for ascending to *power* and the means by which *power* is maintained. Violence, cruelty, and perpetual conflict are deliberately employed, sustaining the divisive anger that entrenches hierarchies and protects the interests of those at the top.

Dangers of Centralized Power

Entrusting *power* to a single, centralized entity significantly magnifies its potential for abuse. Historically and currently, centralized *power* structures tend toward authoritarianism, exploiting social divisions, anger, and fear to consolidate control. Institutions like political movements or authoritarian governments often manipulate societal divisions to cultivate resentment and maintain their dominance. The United States Supreme Court's *Citizens United* ruling exemplifies how concentrated *power* can facilitate the overtaking of democratic processes by wealthy interests, effectively allowing the political system to serve primarily the very affluent. Such developments illustrate vividly the peril inherent in allowing *power* to centralize unchecked, highlighting the urgent need for structures that promote transparency, accountability, and distributed agency.

Impact on the Social Organism

Inverting *power's* potential relational essence disrupts societal harmony and function. Concentrated *power* stratifies society into hierarchical layers, extending from absolute rulers down to marginalized populations, reinforcing systemic inequities. Each echelon experiences limited *liberty*, defined strictly by the boundaries set by those above. This concentration stifles organic feedback, communication, and evolution within the social organism, creating rigidity and brittleness.

Only 80 years after the global victory over fascism, the specter of authoritarianism looms again, underscoring the fragile and continually contested nature of representative and democratic *power* structures. This precarious balance highlights the ever-present risk of returning to oppressive forms of governance, threatening societal cohesion and human dignity.

Potential Restoration

Restoration involves reorienting *power* from vertical dominance to horizontal collaboration. Rather than merely redistributing concentrated *power*, true restoration requires redefining it entirely — as *capacity, agency,* and *shared empowerment*.

Crucially, it also involves the reunification of the people whose collective *power* has been deliberately fragmented. The artificial differences exploited by those in control — differences in race, gender, ethnicity, religion, and class — must be recognized as deliberate manipulations, not inherent divisions.

Restoration means embracing diversity as a source of strength, unifying aspirations around the greater good, and establishing structures that nurture mutual accountability, empathy, and collective well-being. *Power* can only work effectively when it is genuinely inclusive, shared broadly, and operates for the many rather than benefiting solely the top caste. Relationally restored, *power* becomes regenerative, mutually enriching, and resilient, akin to passing a flame from torch to torch without diminishing its brightness.

Authentic restoration demands dismantling dominance paradigms and actively resisting their replication — even within movements striving for equity and liberation. *Power's* relational potential — *trust, stewardship, mutual accountability, unity in diversity* — must become foundational guiding principles.

*From dread to light,
Where only the might
Is to be.*

CHAPTER 14

Recovery
The Breath We Catch

Recovery implies motion after crisis, but too often this word has been twisted to close narratives prematurely — to seal wounds that still bleed, to declare restoration while wreckage remains visible. The chirality of *recovery* reveals itself in how a concept meant to signal healing has been inverted to terminate necessary processes of reckoning and repair.

The term's etymological roots connect to the Old French *recovrer* and Latin *recuperare* — to get back, regain, or restore. Originally, *recovery* signified not merely a return to prior states but a process of reclaiming what had been lost. This meaning carried moral and relational dimensions beyond the mechanical. *Recovery* meant not just functional restoration but the reestablishment of right relationship between parts of a system.

Recovery exists simultaneously across multiple dimensions. It lives in our bodies as the physical processes that restore function after injury. It exists in our psyches as the integration of difficult experiences. It operates in our families as patterns heal or repeat across generations. It functions in our communities as shared traumas are acknowledged and addressed. *Recovery* embodies the capacity to endure — not as mere survival, but as the sustained presence required for genuine transformation.

Throughout American history, *recovery* emerged as a framework following national traumas. After the Civil War, Reconstruction promised a *recovery* that would heal not just economic systems but moral ones — a promise quickly abandoned in favor of restoring antebellum power structures while leaving deeper wounds unaddressed. The pattern repeated through subsequent crises: after economic depressions, natural disasters, social upheavals, and wars, *recovery* increasingly functioned not as genuine healing but as hasty narrative closure.

This inversion accelerated dramatically in recent decades. After September 11th, *recovery* rapidly transformed from a process of collective grief and reflection into the justification for endless war. The language of healing became the language of revenge, all under the banner of *recovery*. After the 2008 financial collapse, *recovery* measured stock market rebounds while millions faced foreclosure without redress.

During the COVID-19 pandemic, *recovery* discourse prioritized market metrics and *returning to normal* over addressing the profound inequities the crisis had exposed and exacerbated.

The dominance paradigm requires this inversion. It needs *recovery* to signal termination rather than transformation. It needs the story to conclude before accountability begins. True *recovery* would require facing what broke and why—an examination the dominance framework cannot tolerate. Instead, *recovery* becomes performance, a ritualized declaration that the discomfort of reckoning has ended whether healing has occurred or not.

In living systems, genuine *recovery* follows different patterns entirely. When forests recover from fire, they do not simply return to previous states. They undergo succession—a complex, multi-stage process where different species perform different functions at different times. Early pioneer species prepare conditions for later ones. The system transforms through *recovery*, becoming something new that incorporates rather than erases the reality of what happened. The forest does not *move on* from the fire; it integrates the burn into its next expression.

Human bodies demonstrate similar wisdom. Healing after serious injury involves not just tissue regeneration but neurological rewiring, compensatory strength building, and psychological adaptation. Nothing simply *returns to normal*. The system transforms through *recovery*, creating new patterns that acknowledge rather than deny the wound.

This inversion affects us most deeply at the communal level, where *recovery* becomes privatized—transformed from a shared process into individual responsibility. When communities experience collective trauma, genuine *recovery* requires collective response. The networks of relationship that sustained harm must be part of restoring wholeness.

True *recovery* acknowledges interdependence rather than isolating pain or resilience. The dominance paradigm fragments this shared dimension, insisting that *recovery* remain a personal burden rather than a communal obligation.

This chapter marks the narrative pivot point—the moment of pause between recognition and response. We have traced the inversions of ten critical words, revealing how language has been twisted to serve dominance rather than connection. Now comes the inhale before deciding what kind of culture might emerge from this recognition.

Recovery does not mean pretending words still carry their original meaning. It does not mean nostalgia for language untainted by power. *Recovery* means creating space to grieve what was lost while refusing the pressure to move on prematurely. It means catching our breath—not to close the story but to begin it anew with clearer vision.

Recovery is not a press release announcing that everything is fine.
It is not a return to normal when normal was the problem.
It is not the absence of discomfort.
It is the space we make for grief to become vision.

For all its apparent strength, the dominance paradigm relies on surprisingly brittle structures: flatten difference, enforce alignment, erase complexity. Its logic is rigid, but life's logic curves, adapts, diverges. Life remembers what dominance tries to erase. It recurs. It surprises. The rigid geometry of control eventually yields to the unpredictable complexity of living systems. If a flower can break through asphalt, we too can breathe, remember, and begin again—not by returning to what was, but by growing toward what might yet be.

CHAPTER 15

Certainty

Once the grounding foundation of trust and stability, now often manipulated into rigidity, exclusion, and dogmatism.

Certainty is commonly perceived as a positive attribute — signifying confidence, clarity, and assurance. Historically, *certainty* provided societies with the stable ground upon which to build trust, relationships, and cohesive communities. It allowed individuals to act decisively, emboldened by a clear vision or deep understanding of shared truths.

Original Meaning
In its original relational form, *certainty* represented trust in shared experience and collective wisdom. Communities found *certainty* through shared narratives, rituals, and mutual agreements, fostering stability and cooperation. *Certainty* was fluid enough to incorporate new information, allowing societies to adapt while maintaining a sense of continuity and security.

Mechanism of Inversion
The inversion of *certainty* emerged when openness and adaptability gave way to rigidity and exclusivity. Dogmatic belief systems, whether religious, ideological, or political, began to leverage *certainty* as an absolute, irrefutable truth. *Certainty* shifted from an evolving, collective agreement to a fixed, imposed reality. This resulted in the end of flexibility, an elimination of doubt, and a calcification of beliefs. Associated beliefs crystallized into dogmatic structures built on false axioms, reducing complex political, philosophical, and psychological ideas into simplistic, rigid truths.

The dominance paradigm appropriated *certainty* to silence doubt, suppress dissent, and marginalize those who questioned established norms. Curiosity diminished, awe faded, and inquisitive doubt was actively discouraged, marking the end of dynamic engagement and intellectual exploration.

This illustrates linguistic chirality clearly: *certainty* retains its form — confidence and assurance — but its orientation reverses from openness and adaptability to rigidity, dogmatism, and inflexible *certainty*.

Current Function

One of the most insidious dangers of *certainty* lies in its natural progression toward oversimplification. What begins as confidence in a shared truth often narrows into reductive binaries, eliminating nuance and muting complexity. This reducibility results in the immobility of ideas — the arrest of intellectual evolution and the paralysis of research. As *certainty* crystallizes into ideology, inquiry becomes a threat rather than a tool. Religious bigotry provides a stark example: where all knowledge is reduced to a handful of fixed axioms, and all investigations are redirected to the sanctioned lore. In such environments, questioning becomes heresy, and dissent is punished not with discourse but with dogma. This trajectory ends not in understanding, but in enforcement — the closing of minds and, historically, the rise of inquisition. The freedom of expression dissolves under the weight of imposed truth, and the very impulse to explore is rendered suspect.

Today, *certainty* often functions as a tool of division rather than cohesion. It underpins polarization, providing the illusion of absolute correctness to opposing sides, each entrenched in their unwavering beliefs. Politically and socially, *certainty* is exploited to deepen divides, justify exclusion, and stifle constructive discourse. *Certainty* becomes weaponized as a form of social control, where deviation from accepted *truths* is not tolerated.

Certainty is also increasingly weaponized against inquiry itself — against questions, investigations, research, and even science. *Certainty* should only come after the scientific process has undeniably verified its theory. With dogma, *certainty* precedes science, to the point of negating it — and, in doing so, ultimately negates itself. The refusal to examine assumptions or tolerate ambiguity has led to public distrust in vital fields of knowledge. Examples include the suppression of stem cell research based on moral absolutism, the rise of the anti-vaccination movement fueled by ideological certitude, and broader cultural backlashes against scientific consensus. In these contexts, the lack of humility that comes with rigid *certainty* becomes a direct threat to human progress.

The damage extends further. *Certainty* in its hardened form diminishes the spark of inspiration. It dulls the inquisitive mind, discourages openness, and weakens tolerance. Most egregiously, it erases humility — the essential humility that recognizes the infinite complexity of the universe, the unresolvable mysteries of consciousness, and the unique, unrepeatable differences between each human being. In place of reverence for the unknown and the unresolved, it installs arrogance and reductionism. *Certainty* replaces the wonder of asking with the finality of pronouncement.

Certainty, divorced from doubt, stifles the very conditions — *curiosity, exploration, open-mindedness* — upon which knowledge and innovation depend. The current use of *certainty* fosters intellectual stagnation and emotional rigidity, limiting society's capacity for growth, innovation, and empathy. Individuals and groups increasingly confine themselves within the narrow bounds of rigidly defined beliefs, unable or unwilling to confront complexity or un*certainty*.

Impact on the Social Organism
The emotional rigidity that often accompanies hardened *certainty* gives rise not only to intellectual stagnation but to a specific, combustible anger. When individuals become wholly identified with their certainties, any challenge is perceived as a personal attack. Those who question or deviate from accepted beliefs are not simply seen as mistaken — they are cast as enemies, threats, or even traitors. Civility vanishes. Friendships erode. Disdain replaces dialogue. The interpersonal cost of *certainty* becomes immense, as the space for empathy and genuine listening is replaced by defensiveness and rage. The anger of *certainty* does not merely protect beliefs — it punishes deviation, building a world where emotional violence precedes understanding, and where ideological loyalty becomes more valued than human connection.

The misuse of *certainty* erodes societal resilience and adaptability, creating brittleness. When *certainty* is enforced as dogma, societies lose their ability to respond flexibly to new challenges, information, or circumstances. Relationships fracture under the weight of uncompromising positions, and collective trust deteriorates. Communities become vulnerable, unable to collaboratively navigate complexity or uncertainty.

The reduction of intellectual curiosity and inquisitive doubt impedes innovation and meaningful dialogue, significantly weakening social cohesion. *Certainty* in its dogmatic form thus represents a profound threat to democratic discourse, diversity, and collective resilience.

Potential Restoration
Restoring *certainty* requires reclaiming its original relational flexibility. *Certainty* must be redefined not as an absolute truth but as shared confidence rooted in collective understanding and trust. Restoration involves actively encouraging doubt, curiosity, and critical questioning as vital elements of healthy societies. It requires dismantling dogmatic beliefs and reintroducing awe and wonder into our engagement with the world.

This involves nurturing environments where doubt and questions are welcomed as opportunities for growth and deeper mutual comprehension. *Certainty*, restored in this way, supports rather than suppresses curiosity, adaptability, and resilience.

Certainty once gentle, threads of trust entwined,
Became rigid armor, excluding the undefined.
Restore its softer voice, a chorus open and free,
Certainty in questions, our shared humanity.

CHAPTER 16

Choice
What Returns When the Loop Is Quiet

Stillness Before Sound
Just as elephants communicate in infrasound, frequencies below human hearing, the dominance paradigm speaks through low-frequency inversions that bypass conscious recognition but still shake the system. The words remain familiar: *freedom, family, security*. The nervous system senses something wrong. The resonance feels off. People grow short-fused, suspicious, reactive without knowing why.

The language sounds accurate yet feels wrong. This represents the somatic consequence of chirality. Like chiral molecules that appear identical but function oppositely, these linguistic inversions vibrate at frequencies our conscious minds miss while our bodies register. The dissonance arrives before we can name it, creating pressure beneath perception that frays coherence from the inside out. Similar to the elephant's rumble traveling through soil and bone rather than air, these inversions propagate not through rational argument but through the connective tissue of culture itself. They move beneath awareness, restructuring our relational architecture while we sleep.

When *freedom and security, family and patriot* all invert along similar patterns simultaneously, no stable reference point exists from which to detect the shift. The ground itself has moved. This explains why conventional critique so often fails. It operates at the frequency of conscious manipulation, of rhetorical devices and propaganda, missing entirely the subliminal rewiring happening at depths our analytical tools were never designed to reach. We require a conceptual seismograph, an instrument calibrated to detect movements at this fundamental level, not merely to disagree with inverted terms but to recognize the pattern of inversion itself.

A moment exists after the rupture, after the naming, after the return of breath, when the system no longer screams. No more noise tries to cover the fracture. No more false certainty echoes in hollow loops. Just a quiet so deep it startles.

The body quiets and the jaw unclenches.
The shoulders drop.

This signifies not resolution but recognition. Not that things are fixed, but that you no longer reside inside the inversion. You observe it from the outside for the first time. The inversions you have tracked, *freedom, order, security, family,* no longer define your horizon. They hover. They linger. Their gravitational pull has weakened. In that stillness, something you forgot begins to stir. Not memory. Not morality. A subtle sense that some things hold while others collapse when touched too closely.

The Shape of Integrity

Long before the body had language, it could discern resonance from dissonance. You knew when something harmonized. You knew when something jarred. Even now, in a world that rewards simulation over substance, your nervous system still knows.

Integrity exists not as a rulebook but as a shape, a rhythm, a return. It manifests as the moment your spine straightens when someone names a truth no one dared speak. It appears as the flutter in your chest when justice lands as more than a slogan. It emerges as the soft breath of relief when *freedom* finally stops meaning permission to dominate. This embodied recognition constitutes our first defense against linguistic chirality. The body knows when a word has twisted even before the mind can name it. This signals the shape of coherence rediscovered, not imposed but remembered. Discernment begins here, not as judgment but as the practice of noticing what no longer fits.

False Loops and Simulated Return

Not all stillness heals. Not every soft voice provides safety. When dominance loses its grip, it rarely retreats. Sometimes it shapeshifts. It cloaks itself in humility. It mimics care. It speaks the language of repair while quietly rerouting the loop back into control. Healing becomes branded. Witness becomes surveillance. Listening becomes data extraction.

Consider diversity initiatives that collect demographic data without redistributing power, or reform programs that measure process improvements while avoiding structural change. These represent chiral simulations, looking like progress while functioning as stasis. You have witnessed an institution praising community healing while mining trauma for PR, a corporation championing equity while hoarding control behind paywalls, a leader invoking dialogue while deleting dissent. Technology accelerates these false returns. Algorithmic feedback loops simulate connection while deepening isolation. The appearance of resonance becomes a product delivered in just-in-time dissonance. These false returns fracture trust while feeding on its residue. Discernment must evolve from passive intuition into practiced alertness, a collective literacy of what resonates as real versus what appears merely rehearsed.

As explored in the sidebar *The Chiral Inversion of a Cry for Justice* (see page 49), the phrase *Black Lives Matter* was not just a cry — it was a choice. A decision to name harm clearly, to act in the face of systemic inversion, and to claim space in a society structured to erase. The phrase *All Lives Matter* positioned itself as more inclusive, but in doing so, revealed the mechanics of a false choice: one that pretends to equalize while deflecting the specific claim that justice requires. This is the hallmark of chiral distortion under the dominance paradigm — when language flips to silence, and neutrality becomes complicity.

The Illusion of Binary Choice
Perhaps the most pervasive false return manifests in how "choice" itself has been inverted. Once celebrated as an emblem of freedom — evidence of autonomy, discernment, and agency — *choice* now often presents itself not as liberation but limitation: a performative selection between two pre-approved options, each shaped by the same underlying paradigm.

The either-or framework that governs contemporary decision-making masquerades as freedom while quietly enforcing constraint. The checklist of pros and cons, the polling booths offering only left or right, Democrat or Republican, Labor or Tory, male or female — each dichotomy reduces the infinite spectrum of human thought and identity into calcified categories. In this narrowed terrain, *choice* no longer expands; it confines.

This is chirality at work: *choice* maintains its surface meaning — volition, selection, empowerment — but its functional orientation has reversed. It now orients away from generativity and toward control. Its logic aligns with the dominance paradigm, which thrives on binaries that erase nuance and flatten difference. In its inverted form, *choice* serves as a gatekeeper, not a gateway.

The cost is subtle yet immense. We lose ambiguity, complexity, elasticity. The fertile imagination of the mind — its ability to hold tension, invent possibility, dance between paradoxes — is replaced by an obsessive demand for clarity, certainty, resolution. This is not clarity in service of truth, but in service of control.

A Choice Without Coercion
Now, quietly, it arrives. Not with thunder or instruction but with invitation. You stand at the fulcrum. One path loops you back into the known. It promises clarity, efficiency, protection from ambiguity. It

rewards proximity to power even as it hollows you. This constitutes the path of simulated return. It costs little up front yet slowly erodes your capacity to feel what resonates as true.

The other path flows more quietly, more slowly. It neither promises comfort nor clarity. It does not perform certainty but simply asks: Can you still feel your own resonance, your own innate tuning fork? This *choice* happens not once but remade with each word spoken, each action taken. It will cost you something—visibility perhaps, advantage, applause. What it gives transcends noise. It returns coherence within and between.

If *choice* is to be restored to its original vitality, it must be reoriented—not a toggle between pre-selected opposites, but a continuum of becoming. A spiral. A constellation. A recognition that true freedom lies not in narrowing possibility to a digestible pair, but in reclaiming the full field of imagination and relation.

In culture, we see signs of this reorientation in the resistance to binary identities. Movements that embrace nonbinary gender expression, hybrid cultural identities, and genre-defying art forms all refuse the reductive either/or in favor of a both/and, or even a neither/nor. The rise of intersectionality as a lens rejects the notion that people must choose which part of their identity "matters most." It insists instead on the validity—and power—of layered complexity.

In politics, the stranglehold of two-party systems is being challenged by calls for ranked-*choice* voting, coalition governance, and participatory democracy. These are not just technical reforms; they represent a shift in the very meaning of political agency—from choosing the lesser evil to articulating collective possibility. The growing disillusionment with traditional party dichotomies reflects a hunger for models of *choice* that invite deliberation, nuance, and multiplicity rather than tribal allegiance.

In psychology, the field is moving away from rigid diagnostic labels and toward trauma-informed, systems-based approaches. Mental states are less often treated as isolated pathologies requiring binary intervention—medicated or not, stable or unstable—and more often understood as complex responses to context, relationship, and history.

Therapeutic models like Internal Family Systems or narrative therapy acknowledge inner multiplicity, encouraging clients to explore a chorus of inner voices rather than suppress all but one.

In each case, the reintegration of *choice* into a relational system—not an adversarial one—restores its vitality. It becomes not a matter of picking a side, but of participating in meaning-making. Not subtraction, but composition. Not exclusion, but connection.

The Quiet of Covenant

If you step toward it, if enough of us do, then something deeper than safety begins to regrow. Not obedience, not ideology, but a covenant sealed not by oath but by presence. This covenant forms not just personally but as the foundation for the regenerative practices that follow, a relational agreement to live inside coherent loops that speaks in resonance, listens with porous attention. It seeks to repair not by erasure but by naming what was torn. This creates a new form of containment, not control but mutual accountability.

You hold the loop for me when I forget.
I hold it for you when you are afraid.
Together, we keep the shape from twisting.

Attunement looks like pausing before reply, naming when harm slips in, letting silence speak where performance once lived. This describes not a campaign but a practice. When enough people choose it, quietly, over and over, the simulation cannot hold. The loop inverts again, this time toward life.

Closing Breath

We were told that freedom meant choosing sides —
left or right, right or wrong, us or them.
But our minds are not levers;
they are landscapes.
There is no liberty in the clenched fist of certainty,
no growth in the soil where only one seed is allowed to root.
Real choice is not a fork in the road,
but the recognition that roads are made,
not found.
It is the whisper between poles,
the spiral between fixed stars,
the quiet defiance of a question unasked.
To choose again
is to refuse the script,
to remember the wild grammar of being,
and to walk — uncertain,
unafraid — into the open field.

The world will not mark the day you made the *choice*, but you will feel it in your breath, in your voice, in the return of your own unbroken name. Not the name dominance handed you or the name algorithm optimized, but the one still tethered to witness, your own and others'.

You did not just choose a path. You chose a practice of coherence in a time of noise. That is how the recursion begins again, this time in trust, we name the wound, and choose to remake our lives honoring the scar that marked our becoming.

CHAPTER 17

News
From Witness to Withhold: How News Becomes Noise

Original Meaning
The word *news* is derived from new — that which is recent, previously unknown, or emerging. It once implied **something worth knowing because it had just come to light.** Historically, *news* was relational: it spread through witness, storytelling, and letters, traveling along human networks of meaning. It was deeply embedded in *the act of noticing and sharing* — an attempt to orient one another within the unfolding present. In this light, *news* served a vital function in the social organism: it was the connective tissue by which communities adapted to change, mourned losses, celebrated births, and responded to danger.

Mechanism of Inversion
The inversion began as technologies of transmission evolved: printing presses, then wire services, broadcast media, and finally the algorithmic superhighways of digital platforms. The *news* became something curated by institutions and eventually optimized by machines. Its original meaning as *relational alert* was displaced by its new role as *currency of attention*. The decanting of *news* — how it rises through editorial ranks — became less about collective significance and more about audience capture. Clickbait replaced clarity. Headlines grew louder while meaning grew thinner.
 In this inverted structure, newness itself became a fetish. Stories with the right *tone, timing, or titillation* rose regardless of substance. Conversely, events of profound consequence could be buried, sidelined, or ignored. *Newsworthiness* was no longer about impact or truth — it was about alignment with trends, narratives, and profitable outrage. Truth became elastic. A worthy story became one that performed well — regardless of whether it *informed*.

Current Function
Today, the word *news* oscillates between authority and parody. It is invoked by both trusted journalism and misinformation campaigns. The same word cloaks exposés of corruption and celebrity feuds. Be-

cause *news* is now primarily an economic function—driven by engagement, shares, and ad revenue—its surface remains identical, even as its *orientation* varies wildly.

This is linguistic chirality: identical form, opposite function. A breaking story may hold truth or serve as narrative weaponry. Its rise through digital channels often reflects *virality*, not veracity. In this environment, *news* is both venerated and distrusted. It is both what people cite as proof and what others denounce as fabrication. Its form is consistent, its effects are divergent.

Impact on the Social Organism

The chiral inversion of *news* corrodes our civic immune system. When the surface markers of legitimacy—datelines, headlines, timestamps—can be applied to any content, the public loses its ability to discern threat from fiction. The social body suffers autoimmune confusion: it attacks truth as falsehood and embraces falsehood as fact.

This also erodes our *attention economy*, training citizens to value novelty over continuity, noise over nuance. A story's power often lasts just long enough to spark outrage or trend online—15 minutes, as Warhol foresaw—before it is replaced by something more clickable. In this state, the *temporarily empowered lie* can do more damage than a *quiet truth* ever has the chance to prevent.

Potential Restoration

To recover *news* from its chiral inversion, we must realign it with its original function: *to bear witness, to orient, to relate*. This means redefining newsworthiness away from *virality* and back toward civic relevance. It requires platforms and institutions that *reward depth over speed, context over spectacle, and truth over trend*.

News could again become a relational act—less about broadcasting and more about stewardship of shared reality. This would require structural changes to how *news* is produced, distributed, and consumed, but also linguistic healing. We must *reclaim* the word *news*—not as a ticker-tape of outrage, but as the pulse of a living democracy.

To notice together is to begin to know.
To know together is to begin to care.
To care together is to begin to change.
Let the news be new again.

THE INTERLUDE

The Shape Beneath the Surface
A pause between distortion and return

This was never written in the usual sense. It was revealed slowly, recursively, with care. Each chapter removed a layer. Each pass cleared a distortion. Not to create something new, but to remember what language sounds like when it is shaped by integrity.

This is not a record of theory. It is the demonstration of a method: recursive, structural, alive. The writing did not just describe the chiral inversions; it enacted the process of seeing them. Each sentence practiced what it asked of the world: containment without collapse, meaning without performance, truth without spectacle.

What emerged was not invention. It was form discovered in tension, revealed by what was carved away. Like a living system recovering its natural orientation after distortion, the text itself has undergone its own recursive correction.

This is not a bridge between chapters. It is the stillness between breath and return. The inhale that follows recognition and precedes action. A moment to notice that the work is no longer just a manuscript. It is a counter-grammar. A resonance chamber. A pattern that remembers how to hold.

Here, we do not press forward. We pause to witness what has been revealed. To hear the echo that answers back, not as noise, but as fidelity.

The Recursion Arc
Moving Beyond "Seen"

CHAPTER 19

The Chirality of News
From Fetish to Fourth Estate

Imagine that... (The Inversion)
Technologies of transmission are just beginning to evolve—first the printing press, then the wire service, followed by radio, television, and now the algorithmic instantaneity of digital platforms. Imagine that *news*—once a living signal passed between people who noticed and cared—now becomes something curated by institutions, then fine-tuned by machines. Its original role as relational alert fades, and in its place emerges a new currency: attention. The process by which a story rises—once rooted in relevance and shared meaning—shifts toward performance metrics and audience capture. Clarity gives way to clickbait. Headlines get louder. Everything is Breaking News. Meaning evaporates.

Now, imagine that newness itself turns into a fetish. Stories that hit the right tone, ride the right timing, or promise just the right thrill float to the top—no matter their substance. Meanwhile, events of deep consequence—slow-moving, complex, or inconvenient—are sidelined, buried, or simply ignored. The measure of newsworthiness no longer rests on truth or impact, but on alignment with fashion, narrative, and outrage that can be monetized. In this world, truth bends. A worthy story becomes one that performs—not one that informs.

Imagine further that the very idea of a shared public reality begins to dissolve. Information silos proliferate. Micro-journalists and influencers flood the ecosystem with commentary disguised as coverage, each feeding niche audiences what they want to hear. Echo chambers become echo markets. Trust fragments. *News*, once a plural conversation grounded in verification, becomes a stream of monologues engineered for loyalty rather than learning. In this chiral distortion, the truth becomes not merely contested—but optional.

Imagine that... (The Recovery)
Now imagine *news* recovering itself—not as nostalgia, not as myth, but as a renewed civic force. A plural press, rich in perspectives but united by standards, emerges as a resilient immune system for democracy. Its value lies not in speed, but in synthesis, not in prov-

ocation, but in proportion. Journalists are neither demagogues nor background noise — they are interpreters, grounded in discipline, humility, and the ethics of verification.

Imagine an environment where the influence of radicalized reporting and partisan distortion begins to weaken — not through censorship, but through *trust restored*. Where diverse outlets compete not for outrage but for insight. Where the work of reporting outpaces the race for reaction. In such a landscape, micro-journalism still exists but is contextualized by institutions that hold the line — fact-checking, pattern-detecting, signal-seeking amidst the noise.

Now imagine that this recovery is not dependent on heroic figures or messianic anchors. We do not need another Cronkite cult or Murrow mythology — we need the ethos they embodied to be *distributed*. Trust does not reside in personality but in process. The story matters more than the storyteller — but the storyteller's integrity is what ensures the story's fidelity. Transparency replaces charisma. Accountability replaces access.

Imagine that readers, too, recover their role — not as passive consumers of sensation, but as participants in a democratic feedback loop. A civically engaged public doesn't just demand good journalism — it *sustains* it. Subscribes to it. Defends it. Participates in the ecology of facts, nuance, and debate. And in turn, the press becomes not a fading institution, but a living membrane — a filter and mirror, a pulse and conscience.

In this reorientation, *news* is no longer a fleeting moment of virality. It is a structure of coherence — a scaffolding that helps us build meaning across difference, across time. The Fourth Estate is no longer a slogan — it is a function. Not above or apart from society but *interwoven* with it. Its purpose is not to dominate the discourse, but to deepen it.

Imagine that the news is new again
— not because it's novel,
but because it's trustworthy.

CHAPTER 20

Regeneration
The Work of Becoming

*R*egeneration is not a reset. It is not a return. It is the slow, cellular work of becoming something new — something that remembers the wound, the scar, the trace of the choice that illuminates the path ahead that will allow us to live in alignment. Where recovery pauses, *regeneration* begins. It is not performative. It is not linear. It is recursive, alive, adaptive. It requires us to become stewards of meaning, to protect language from further distortion, because the dominance paradigm hasn't disappeared. It remains actively at work.

Dominance is the mechanism that forced chirality to poison everything it has already twisted, continues to twist, and seeks relentlessly to keep twisting. This is not a historical artifact but an active force — a present and persistent pressure constantly working to invert meaning for the sake of maintaining control.

The dominance paradigm reversed the moral current of our language, transformed care into control, made strength out of cruelty. It trained us to speak with the syntax of fear. In this pause between exhale and inhale, between recognition and response, we must see more clearly what has happened. The inversions we've traced in these ten words — *freedom, order, patriot, family, security, innocence, reform, efficiency, diversity, recovery* — aren't isolated shifts. They aren't separate territories of meaning that somehow, coincidentally, all underwent similar transformations.

Some might frame these as distinct moral domains or foundations — *care, fairness, loyalty, authority, sanctity, liberty* — each with its own evolutionary history and psychological function. Such segmentation misses the deeper pattern. These aren't separate muscles that independently weakened or failed. They are expressions of a more fundamental relational fabric that has been systematically rewoven.

This relational fabric constitutes the invisible infrastructure of shared meaning that makes civic life possible. It comprises the threads of trust between speakers and listeners, the mutual expectations that words will carry stable meanings, the shared commitment to truth-telling even across difference. The fabric includes our collective capacity to distinguish fact from fiction, to navigate complexity without collapse, to negotiate meaning without domination. Most importantly, it includes our faith that language serves connection rather than control—that words build bridges rather than barriers.

The dominance paradigm doesn't target individual concepts one by one. It transforms the entire relational field in which all meaning exists. It alters the very sinew that connects our moral vocabulary—the underlying infrastructure of how we relate to each other, to truth, and to power.

This explains why the same pattern of inversion appears across such diverse domains, why freedom and security, innocence and order all twisted in the same direction, serving the same function. They were captured not concept-by-concept but through a transformation of the relational medium in which they exist.

Regeneration begins when we name that mechanism and refuse it. This is why the practices that follow aren't attempts to reclaim individual words. We aren't offering ten separate remedies for ten separate inversions. What follows is a unified approach to healing the relational infrastructure beneath all of them. Relational language cannot survive in a dominance frame. It needs space. It needs consent. It needs correction, repetition, tending.

Similar to mycelium after a forest fire, linguistic *regeneration* begins with fragile threads of connection. After devastating burns, fungal networks don't immediately rebuild the entire forest ecosystem. They start with microscopic filaments that slowly reconnect separated areas, gradually building complexity and resilience. The process is tentative, vulnerable, yet incredibly persistent. These fungal networks transmit nutrients, share information about threats, and ultimately create the conditions for new growth.

Our work of linguistic *regeneration* follows this same pattern. We cannot immediately reclaim all inverted terms simultaneously. Instead, we must patiently establish small networks of meaning, create protected spaces where words maintain their integrity, and gradually expand these zones of coherence. One connection leads to another. The network grows stronger, more resilient. While we may not retake the whole forest at once, we can tend the soil. We can begin again with words that heal.

This work stands neither conservative nor progressive in the conventional sense. It doesn't seek merely to restore original meanings, nor simply to create new language. It aims to heal the connective tissue that makes genuine moral discourse possible across difference. None of us can walk this path alone well. The *regeneration* of meaning requires collective practice, mutual witnessing, shared stewardship. Only through relational effort can we restore the fabric that has been systematically unraveled.

Regeneration is the long work. It is quiet and difficult. It requires persistence in the face of resistance, community in the face of isolation, hope in the face of cynicism. It is also the only real path forward. To live in a democracy, we must speak in one, and that means learning, again, what our words are made to carry.

CHAPTER 21

The Other Hand of Power
Power as Conduction, Not Control

Original Meaning
In its earliest conception, *power* was not synonymous with rule. It was not clenched in fists or enshrined in thrones. Instead, it denoted potential — the ability to do, to act, to bring something into being. The Latin *potere*, from which the word *power* originates, speaks to this generative capacity. It is kin to the word *potent*, meaning capable, alive with possibility.

In living systems, this form of *power* is visible everywhere. It is in the ability of fungi to transmit nutrients between trees across a vast mycelial network. It is in the coordinated, leaderless motion of starlings in murmuration, each bird responding to the seven nearest others, forming a unified whole without a central command. It is in the pulse of the heart, which beats not in isolation but in dialogue with the breath and the brain.

This is the kind of *power* that sustains life. It does not dominate — it synchronizes. It does not conquer — it coheres. It is not loud, but it is unrelenting. In its presence, systems find their rhythm, communities find their voice, and action finds its direction.

Mechanism of Inversion
The chirality of *power* emerges when this relational, life-affirming potential is turned against itself — when the hand that could offer becomes a fist. Under the dominance paradigm, *power* was pried from its embeddedness in relationship and recast as a force to be wielded from above.

Its orientation flipped. Rather than *with*, *power* became over. Rather than nourishing, it began to extract.

This inversion was neither accidental nor neutral. It accompanied and enabled the rise of imperial states, patriarchal hierarchies, racial caste systems, slavery, and capitalist economies of accumulation. Wherever *power* became something to own rather than share, its function shifted.

What had once flowed through relationship was redirected into architecture: towers, borders, weapons, chains. Strength became synonymous with control; influence became indistinguishable from coercion.

The inversion of *power* separated the capacity to act from the responsibility to care. It severed strength from stewardship, decisiveness from listening, agency from consequence.

Current Function (of Recovered Power)

Yet even under the weight of this inversion, the original frequency of *power* persists — often muffled, but never extinguished. Across movements for justice, models of distributed leadership, and experiments in collaborative governance, we are witnessing the reemergence of *power* as a *shared capacity,* rather than a solitary possession.

This restored *power* does not look like charisma or dominance. It moves through trust, responsiveness, and mutual recognition. It expresses itself in contexts where people are empowered not through fear or hierarchy, but through clarity, care, and meaningful participation.

It is visible in the teacher who shapes a classroom through empathy and curiosity, not control. In the cooperative that distributes profits equitably among its members. In the open-source software community that maintains systems relied upon by millions without centralized authority.

These are not marginal anomalies; they are harbingers of a different orientation. In this recovered state, *power* feels like integrity moving outward — it aligns means with ends. It enhances agency while preserving relationship. It expands what is possible without narrowing who belongs.

Impact on the Social Organism

When *power* reverts to its original form, the social body reorganizes itself. Structures loosen, not into chaos, but into adaptability. Rigid hierarchies soften into networks of trust. Civic life becomes breathable again. This transformation is not merely political — it is physiological. Just as trauma compresses the nervous system and inhibits flow, corrupted *power* constricts the body politic. Restored *power* releases this tension. It allows institutions to breathe, individuals to contribute meaningfully, and ideas to evolve in dialogue rather than in echo chambers or edicts.

A culture rooted in relational *power* does not mistake control for safety or obedience for harmony. It recognizes that coherence emerges not from sameness, but from resonance. That difference is not a threat, but a necessity for vitality. That strength, to be sustainable, must be reciprocal.

Potential Restoration

To restore *power* in its right orientation is to reintroduce the conditions under which it becomes a force for flourishing. It begins not with structural overhaul, but with a change in stance — a reorientation of intent.

We must begin by asking different questions. Not "How can I get others to do what I want?" but "What wants to happen through us?" Not "How can we ensure compliance?" but "How can we foster coherence?" The restoration of *power* requires replacing the architecture of domination with the grammar of relationship.

In education, this means shifting from top-down instruction to project-based learning, that cultivates inquiry, autonomy, and critical thinking. The goal is not to produce obedient workers, but to raise generative thinkers — people capable of acting in the world with discernment and care — people who will contribute rather than repeat.

In governance, it means designing systems that listen as much as they legislate. Democracy, at its best, is not merely a method of decision-making — it is a method of *power-sharing*, of weaving accountability through participation. When decisions are made in rooms that echo with many voices, rather than just the loudest, *power* becomes less brittle, more durable, and more legitimate.

In business, restoration involves turning away from extractive metrics and toward regenerative models. Leadership no longer means climbing above others; it means becoming a node through which vision, resources, and purpose can flow. It means recognizing that organizations are not machines to be optimized, but organisms to be nurtured.

Even in language, we must restore *power* by changing how we speak. We must resist the reduction of complex realities into binary slogans. We must reclaim nuance, invite paradox, and learn to speak not to win, but to understand.

Restored *power* does not abolish leadership; it dignifies it. It transforms leadership from authority into responsibility, from command into composition. It insists that to lead is not to control the current, but to sense it, shape it, and flow with it toward what serves the whole.

Above all, restoration means returning to the idea that *power* is not what lifts one above others — it is what lifts us all. That when *power* is shared, it expands. When it is grounded, it grows. When it is trusted, it transforms.

True power does not announce itself. It hums — quiet, steady, and alive. It tunes itself to the needs of the moment, the call of the collective, the arc of becoming.

*It does not rise above — it rises through.
Like roots. Like rhythm. Like breath.*

CHAPTER 22

Listening
The First Practice of Return

Before language carries thought, *listening* makes room for meaning to take shape. Not as absence but as presence, *listening* creates the space where understanding begins. This first practice of regeneration invites us to return to our bodies — to the wisdom that precedes words.

The dominance paradigm trains our nervous systems toward constant vigilance, toward scanning rather than receiving. Our shoulders tense. Our jaws tighten. Our breath becomes shallow — preparing always for response rather than allowing ourselves to be changed by what we hear. This embodied state makes genuine *listening* impossible. We hear only threats or confirmations, filtering all else as irrelevant.

True *listening* begins with a physiological shift — a conscious relaxing of the guard. The shoulders drop. The jaw softens. The breath deepens and slows. This isn't metaphorical but literal — a tangible surrender of the defensive posture dominance requires. From this state, we can begin to receive without immediate categorization, without instant judgment of usefulness or threat.

When we listen from embodied presence, we feel language differently. The words *freedom* or *security* land not just as concepts but as lived experiences with somatic signatures. We can sense when a term has twisted away from its relational purpose, not through abstract analysis but through the body's immediate recognition of dissonance. Something feels off — not intellectually wrong but viscerally misaligned.

This capacity for embodied discernment has been systematically diminished. From classrooms where children must sit still to workplaces where emotion signals unprofessionalism, institutional structures train us away from somatic wisdom. We learn to override the body's signals, to privilege disembodied reasoning over integrated knowing. The resulting disconnection makes us vulnerable to linguistic manipulation — unable to sense when meaning has inverted.

Listening as regenerative practice requires reclaiming this connection. It asks us to trust the stomach tightening when someone speaks of *freedom* while advocating control. To notice the chest constriction when *security* is used to justify fear. To feel the throat closing when *family* becomes weapon rather than shelter. These responses aren't distractions from understanding but essential components of it — the body's recognition of linguistic chirality.

Creating space for this embodied *listening* means slowing down. It means allowing pauses that might feel uncomfortable at first — gaps where meaning can settle beyond the rapid-fire exchange dominance values. These pauses aren't empty; they're fertile. In the silence between words, integration happens. Connections form. Understanding deepens not through acceleration but through resonance.

The practice begins with yourself. Notice what happens in your body when you speak. Where does tension arise? What emotions surface? Which topics create constriction? These patterns reveal where dominance has shaped your relationship with language — where you've learned to perform rather than express, to control rather than connect.

Then expand this awareness to exchanges with others. What happens in your nervous system during conversation? Do you listen to respond or to understand? Can you feel the difference between these states? When someone speaks difficult truth, can you stay present with the discomfort rather than rushing to ease it? These questions aren't abstract inquiries but invitations to embodied practice.

In groups and communities, *listening* requires creating containers strong enough to hold difference without collapsing into either false harmony or destructive conflict. Indigenous practices offer guidance — talking circles that pass objects signifying the right to speak, ensuring each voice receives undivided attention before response begins. These aren't merely procedures but embodied technologies for creating shared presence across difference.

Digital environments present particular challenges to embodied *listening*. Screens flatten the multidimensional cues that help us attune to each other. Text removes tone, facial expression, and the subtle shifts that signal emotional states. Platforms accelerate exchange beyond the body's integration capacity. Yet even here, we can practice intentional slowing, conscious breathing, attention to our physical responses as we read and write.

Listening reaches beyond human exchange to include attunement with the more-than-human world. The rustle of leaves, the quality of silence before storm, the tension in animals sensing danger — these communications contain wisdom our linguistic frameworks struggle to incorporate.

Indigenous traditions developed practices for attending to these signals, recognizing that human language alone provides insufficient understanding of complex living systems.

In a culture that valorizes declaration, *listening* becomes radical practice. It creates space for voices systematically silenced. It holds room for meanings power would prefer to erase. It allows complexity to exist without premature resolution. This isn't passive reception but active creation of the conditions where new understanding might emerge.

When enough people practice embodied *listening*, something shifts. Conversations slow down enough for nuance to surface. Opposing perspectives find unexpected common ground. New meanings emerge that weren't visible from either polarized position. The fabric of shared understanding — torn by dominance's inversions — begins to mend not through force but through genuine reception.

Listening is not waiting for your turn to speak.
It is not scanning for points to counter.
It is not strategic extraction.
It is the embodied courage to be changed by what you hear.

CHAPTER 23

Witness
Beyond Neutrality's Collapse

Witness is presence without intrusion. It is holding what is real without turning away. Under the dominance paradigm, even this fundamental act of seeing clearly underwent a chiral inversion. Nowhere is that transformation more evident than in journalism.

Once a steward of public truth, journalism became something else: a performance of neutrality, a choreography of access. The press was meant to bear *witness* to power, not bend to it. The gravitational pull of dominance gradually collapsed that structure from within. This transformation had historical roots. During the Cold War, American media evolved from overtly political to ostensibly objective. This shift occurred not organically through natural evolution but through active shaping by government interests. Organizations like Radio Free Europe operated with secret CIA funding through the 1960s and into the 1970s, blurring the lines between journalism and propaganda.

Media consolidation into fewer corporate hands through the 1980s and 1990s fragmented the shared reference points that once united Americans. The common information environment that allowed for collective *witness* dissolved. Today's media landscape, with its infinite customization, allows people to inhabit entirely separate realities. It functions as a black hole for truth.

Facts cannot escape the event horizon of false equivalence. Accountability becomes flattened into *both sides*. The pursuit of objectivity functions as a muzzle, stripping journalists of their moral clarity while elevating those who lie the loudest. Spectacle replaces substance. Ratings replace rigor. Access replaces truth. Trust undergoes not merely damage but complete devourment, unraveling something larger: the public's ability to share reality.

When *witness* inverts, distortion becomes default. Those who try to speak clearly receive the label of *biased* because clarity itself becomes suspicious in a dominance system. The digital acceleration of this process manifests as breathtaking; what once took decades now happens in moments as language compresses into ever-briefer forms that strip away context and nuance.

Witness begins as a personal practice before it becomes a professional one. It requires cultivating attention that doesn't flinch from discomfort or seek immediate resolution. When someone shares pain, *witness* means staying present without rushing to fix, advise, or relate it back to our own experience. It means hearing words not just for their literal content but for the emotional truth they carry. Professional witnesses—journalists, documentarians, therapists—formalize what we all must learn: that staying with difficult realities is how we begin to transform them.

Witnessing in a dominance culture requires courage. It means seeing injustice even when acknowledging it might cost us. It means noticing linguistic drift even when naming it marks us as *divisive*. Without this willingness to see clearly, no repair remains possible. We cannot heal what we refuse to *witness*.

To regenerate our civic imagination, we must first restore this capacity: to *witness* without collapsing the truth. Real witnessing exists not as passive observation but as a relational act. It affirms presence. It sees harm without flinching and names what dominance tries to blur.

We begin again by reclaiming this role, not just for journalists, but for all of us. In the face of engineered inversion, every act of *witness* represents resistance, and every resistance illuminates truth against the gravitational warping of what we know.

Truth still lives—but it needs eyes that do not flinch, do not look away, and never confuse truth with power.

CHAPTER 24

Naming
When Truth Becomes Visible

Naming is not labeling. It is not categorization. It is the act of making meaning visible — of drawing something out from ambiguity into relational clarity. In the beginning was the word, and *naming* is how we shape our worlds.

Dominance relies on euphemism, deflection, and coded language. It twists meanings to hide power. It calls exploitation opportunity and extraction development. It labels resistance disorder and submission peace. Regeneration begins when we name things honestly. Not cruelly. Not loudly, but truly.

The Ancient Practice of Calling Forth

Throughout human history, *naming* has been a sacred act. Indigenous cultures worldwide recognize *naming* ceremonies as thresholds of becoming. To be named is to be recognized; to name is to create relationship. The power to name has always been the power to make visible, to call into being, to acknowledge existence.

This fundamental human practice existed long before written language. Our ancestors named the stars, the seasons, the patterns of migration. They named their children, their tools, their fears. Each act of *naming* created a shared reference point, a way to coordinate meaning across minds and generations.

In healthy systems, *naming* enables repair. When something is named accurately, it can be addressed directly. Pain can be treated, injustice confronted, beauty celebrated.

But in dominance systems, *naming* triggers removal. Those who name inconvenient truths often find themselves removed instead of the problems they identified. This is one of the quietest inversions of all. And one of the most dangerous.

The Inversion of Meaning

In the dominance paradigm, language is often preserved in form while reversed in function. This is chirality at the level of communication — words like *alignment, collaboration,* or *shared values* that once pointed to mutual clarity are now used to mask *power,* filter *dissent,* and displace *challenge.*

These terms don't lose their dictionary definitions; they lose their operational integrity. That's far more insidious because the words still sound ethical. They still look inclusive, but in use, they become tools of *compliance*.

The chiral twist occurs when *naming* — once a practice of clarification and mutual understanding — becomes classified as disruption or disloyalty. The same act that builds relational coherence in healthy systems becomes grounds for exclusion in dominance frameworks. The shape of the practice remains identical while its functional meaning reverses entirely.

When language turns, trust breaks. And when trust breaks, it becomes harder and harder to name what's happening at all — especially from inside the system.

Naming in Living Systems

In ecological systems, *naming* manifests as recognition — the capacity to identify patterns that signal health or disease. When forests encounter pathogens, mycorrhizal networks transmit chemical signals that *name* the threat, allowing the system to respond. This *naming* doesn't create division; it enables collective response.

Similarly, our bodies contain sophisticated *naming* mechanisms. Immune cells identify foreign particles through molecular recognition — a biological *naming* process that distinguishes self from non-self. When this system functions properly, it protects the whole. When it malfunctions, autoimmune disorders develop, with the body attacking itself based on mistaken *naming*.

The dominance paradigm creates similar autoimmune responses in social systems. Accurate *naming* gets labeled as the disease rather than the diagnosis. The system attacks those who identify problems rather than addressing the problems themselves.

The Pattern of Silencing

This pattern repeats across institutions of all kinds. External partners brought into organizations to drive change often experience it most acutely. Initially welcomed as catalysts for transformation, their work may show promising results that leadership celebrates. But systems resistant to genuine change often respond predictably when these partners move beyond surface improvements to identify deeper structural issues.

As organizational leadership shifts, the rhetoric frequently softens while control mechanisms harden. Existing power structures rarely dissolve; they simply reposition beneath new titles and frameworks. Terms like *alignment, team culture,* and *shared values* begin to circulate — not as invitations to coherence but as tools for containment. Those without formal protections within the organization become particularly vulnerable.

When these partners name the drift — when they highlight quiet consolidations of power, fraying ethical commitments, or widening gaps between stated values and actual practices — they rarely receive engagement with the substance of their concerns. Instead, they face progressive distancing, strategic silence, and eventually displacement. This removal rarely stems from failure of the work itself, but from the inconvenience of their clarity.

The pattern reveals how *naming* functions differently in dominance versus relational systems. What should trigger repair instead triggers removal. The identification of problems becomes classified as the problem, while the issues themselves remain unaddressed. Those who believed they were invited to transform find they were merely expected to perform. *Naming* operates at every level of society. In families, it's the ability to identify patterns without being labeled 'too sensitive.' In workplaces, it's the capacity to identify ethical breaches without being dismissed as 'not a team player.' In democracies, it's the freedom to identify corruption without being branded 'unpatriotic.'

The dominance paradigm relies on our hesitation to name what we see. It counts on euphemism replacing precision, on comfort outweighing courage. But *naming* is not an attack — it is an act of profound optimism. It says: I believe that seeing clearly together is possible. I believe repair is worth attempting. I believe truth matters not because it punishes, but because it heals.

Euphemism as Policy

This is how dominant systems protect themselves: Not by resolving tension, but by reframing it as misalignment. Not by facing correction, but by removing the witness. Alignment becomes a shield against discomfort. Culture fit becomes a proxy for sameness. Collaboration becomes a euphemism for deference, and excellence — particularly the kind that doesn't orbit hierarchy — gets filtered out through HR language dressed as professionalism.

Consider how often the most innovative voices are labeled not a team player or difficult to work with when their real offense is refusing to participate in collective avoidance. A designer who insists on user feedback before approving a product. A teacher who documents how a new policy harms vulnerable students. A nurse who reports safety violations that management finds inconvenient to address.

That's the chirality. That's the twist. Terms that should protect quality become weapons that eliminate it. This isn't about individual managers or bad intentions. It's about structural conditions that punish integrity while rewarding performative compliance.

We Name Because We Care

This is why we've taken the Workplace Psychological Safety Pledge, and why we proudly support the Workplace Psychological Safety Act (wpsact.org), because *naming* harm is not disruption—it is the first act of repair. And when systems punish those who name, they are not defending values. They are defending a comfort zone built on avoidance.

We believe psychological safety must extend beyond payroll. Contractors, collaborators, and community partners all deserve protection when *naming* harm. All deserve to be heard without retaliation, because language only retains its integrity when it protects those who use it to tell the truth.

Naming is clarity. *Naming* is accountability. *Naming* is the moment a broken pattern becomes visible. To name the mechanism that twisted language is to break its spell. To name what hurts, to name what heals, to name what was taken—this is how culture reorients. It is how we find our way back to breath.

Naming as Covenant

In a dominance system, *naming* is framed as antagonism. In a relational system, *naming* is a gift. It says: I see the breach, and I care enough to make it visible. It says: I trust that this can be corrected—if we're willing to face it. It says: I'm still here. That's what makes *naming* sacred, and that's why the power to name must be stewarded—not just preserved, but protected from inversion. When we lose the ability to name what's breaking, we lose the possibility of repair.

Naming is not a threat. It is an invitation, and that invitation is what true alignment actually means. Not conformity. Not quiet compliance. Not comfort at the cost of truth.

Alignment means choosing to stand inside the integrity of what we've named—even when it's hard, even when it's not rewarded. It means tethering our language to our values, our actions to our care, and our systems to the people they claim to serve. Alignment is not the absence of conflict. It is the presence of courage.

When we reclaim *naming* from the empire of misdirection, we recover the first right of voice. We restore precision to speech. We make visible what dominance concealed, because *naming* is only the beginning. Living in alignment with what we've named is where integrity begins.

Naming is not attack.
It is not defiance.
It is not disruption.
It is the first breath of repair.

CHAPTER 25

Consent
The Boundary That Heals

Consent once lived at the heart of civic exchange. It signaled mutual ground, shared understanding, agreement that could hold weight. It marked the sacred space where minds could meet in honest recognition.

From village councils to constitutional assemblies, the idea that meaning requires mutual agreement predates modern democracy. Tribal elders sought consensus before action. Early republics required citizen assent for legitimate governance. The Haudenosaunee Confederacy established decision-making protocols requiring attentive listening until genuine accord emerged. *Consent* wasn't just permission; it was relationship.

This understanding has undergone a profound inversion.

In the dominance paradigm, communication transforms into extraction: say what I want, when I want it, on my terms regardless of impact. Information becomes power. Disclosure becomes forced. Story becomes weaponized.

This is the chirality of *consent*. The same basic shape functioned in opposite ways based on orientation within power structures.

Where genuine *consent* creates mutual ground for exchange, its inverted form creates terrain for conquest. The dominance mechanism requires this inversion. It needs *consent* to become compliance rather than choice. It needs permission to become formality rather than relationship. It needs exchange to become extraction rather than reciprocation.

We see this inversion operating across systems.

In media, attention is harvested without meaningful choice through design intended to override conscious decision-making.

In governance, complex policies hide behind impenetrable language and "I agree" buttons, rendering *consent* meaningless while maintaining its form.

In education, students are required to speak but rarely asked if they're ready to be heard.

In technology, terms of service stretch thousands of words, ensuring *consent* exists as legal protection rather than authentic understanding.

Similar to other inverted terms we've examined, *consent* maintains its familiar outline while its effects have completely reversed. What once established ground for mutual exchange now functions as shield for unilateral extraction. The twisted form serves power while appearing to protect autonomy.

This inversion disrupts our collective ability to create meaning together.

Consent becomes simulated rather than authentic, causing language itself to fracture. We cannot build shared understanding when the very foundation of exchange—willful participation—has been corrupted.

The consequences ripple through civic life. Communities lose the muscle memory of genuine negotiation. Organizations forget that authentic buy-in requires more than signatures. Digital spaces replace relational *consent* with algorithmic prediction, not asking what we want but inferring it based on patterns, a simulation that further erodes our experience of genuine choice.

The body knows this difference.

Consent becomes authentic when something in the nervous system settles. The shoulders drop. The breath deepens. The mind clears.

Consent becomes coerced when the opposite occurs. Subtle vigilance activates. A low-grade tension signals manipulation even before consciousness names it.

Consent disrupts the dominance pattern. It restores mutuality to meaning. It reestablishes the relational foundation that language requires to function as connection rather than control.

Genuine *consent* says: May I ask? May I share this story? Are you ready for this truth?

It recognizes that words have impact, that they land in nervous systems, not just in minds. It quiets coercion. It rebuilds trust where intrusion has reigned. It creates the conditions for honest exchange.

Relational *consent* manifests differently across contexts. In journalism, it means transparency about the impact of difficult news rather than ambushing audiences with trauma. In education, it means creating genuine space for students to decline participation without penalty when content touches personal wounds. In governance, it means ensuring policy language is genuinely accessible, not just technically public. In digital spaces, it means design that enhances conscious choice rather than exploiting unconscious patterns.

In regenerative language, *consent* becomes a baseline ethic. A culture where permission is respected becomes a culture where voices rise without fear, where stories unfold without exploitation, where truth emerges without coercion.

This connects directly to the practices of naming and witness that precede it, and prepares the ground for tending and reciprocation that follow.

Reclaiming *consent* requires recognizing how fundamental it is to linguistic integrity. We create conditions for language that heals rather than harms, that connects rather than controls, that serves life rather than dominance when we speak and listen with *consent* at the center.

Consent is not a checkbox.
It is not a formality.
It is not a barrier.
It is the space we hold for each other's dignity.

CHAPTER 26

Tending
The Patience of Renewal

Tending exists as the antithesis of conquest. It embodies slowness, subtlety, and commitment to remain present. Language functions not as an instrument awaiting endless sharpening but as a garden, a commons, a living ecosystem requiring cultivation.

The practice of *tending* involves noticing the moment meaning begins to unravel. It requires pruning distortion before proliferation occurs. It demands fertilizing forgotten words, watering clarity, weeding out the inversions introduced by the dominance paradigm before they normalize within our discourse.

Dominant culture valorizes speed above all else. Acceleration represents progress. Extraction signifies success. *Tending* resists these assumptions fundamentally. It returns us to appropriate pace, to specific place, to authentic care.

The *tending* of language involves persistent questioning: Does this word maintain alignment with its purpose? Does it continue serving connection? Has it undergone capture by systems of power? Has it drifted from its relational essence? The languages that endure through generations are those someone loved enough to tend with deliberate attention.

This practice operates at multiple scales simultaneously. Individual speakers tend language through precise usage and careful listening.

Communities tend shared vocabularies through honest dialogue about contested terms. Institutions tend linguistic ecosystems through policies that value clarity over obfuscation. Each scale requires different techniques but shares the same fundamental orientation toward care rather than control.

Unlike the inversions we have traced, *tending* carries no pretense of efficiency. It embraces the slow work of cultivation, recognizing that genuine coherence cannot be manufactured or imposed but must be grown over time.

The dominance paradigm rushes language toward predetermined outcomes. *Tending* allows meaning to emerge through relationship, at*tending* to the conditions that foster linguistic integrity without forcing specific forms.

Tending is not control.
It is not perfection.
It is not purification.
It is the daily work of keeping language alive.

The responsive rhythms of *tending* stand in direct contrast to the extractive patterns of dominance. Where dominance depletes meaning for immediate advantage, *tending* enriches the soil in which future understanding might grow. This represents not just semantic stewardship but democratic necessity, for a people who cannot tend shared language cannot govern themselves across difference.

CHAPTER 27

Reciprocation
The Sacred Circle of Exchange

Reciprocation forms the heartbeat of relational language, creating a steady rhythm of giving and receiving that pulses through our cultural body. The dominance paradigm speaks to overpower, to dominate, to win; it monologues, interrupts, and demands while treating language as a weapon rather than a bridge. Its words land like stones, expecting nothing in return except submission.

Relational speech moves in cycles instead. It listens, reflects, and builds coherence between speaker and listener, creating an ecosystem rather than a hierarchy. Each utterance contains within it the invitation for response — not merely reaction but genuine engagement. This ancient pattern predates written language itself, emerging from our earliest gatherings around fires where stories circled like embers, each voice kindling the next.

Reciprocation does not always require agreement, yet remains grounded in regard. It restores the understanding that meaning emerges together rather than being imposed from above. It reminds us that language evolved primarily to connect, not to conquer — to coordinate collective action, to share vital information, to weave the social fabric that ensured our survival.

The digital transformation of communication has further accelerated the inversion of reciprocity. Platforms designed as *social* media often function as broadcast mechanisms, their algorithms rewarding monologue over dialogue, dopamine over reflection. This is not accidental architecture but deliberate design that treats attention as resource rather than relationship.

Words flow in patterns mimicking exchange while actually functioning as extraction — of data, of engagement, of the very capacity for sustained conversation.

Consider how often digital *conversations* devolve into parallel monologues, each voice speaking past the others, less interested in understanding than in being heard. This pattern replicates across contexts: in classrooms where questioning becomes threatening rather than deepening; in workplaces where feedback flows only downward; in governance where citizen input becomes performative rather than informative.

When language becomes genuinely reciprocal, it transforms into a site of trust—a space where people can meet not to win but to witness each other into being. The linguistic field shifts from battlefield to commons, from contest to cultivation. Words travel like roots underground, connecting separate beings into a living network that sustains all participants.

In healthy living systems, *reciprocation* is not merely ethical but functional. Forests thrive through mycorrhizal networks where trees exchange carbon for minerals, where information about threats passes from plant to plant. These systems derive their resilience not from dominance but from constant, calibrated exchange. Our languages once operated similarly, each voice adjusting to make room for others, the meaning emerging not from any single speaker but from the interaction between them.

Reciprocation transcends mere transaction.
It surpasses simple score-keeping.
It exceeds the logic of demand.
It embodies the sacred circle of language exchanged with care.

To regenerate reciprocal speech requires practical rituals: speaking with questions that invite genuine response; reading to understand before reading to refute; allowing silence to be pregnant rather than empty; practicing the delicate art of turn-taking that makes room without reservation. These ancient technologies of conversation still live in our cultural memory, waiting to be reclaimed.

The dominance paradigm would have us believe that communication functions linearly—from powerful to powerless, from knower to learner, from center to margin. But words were never meant to travel in straight lines. They spiral, circle, return. They echo and ripple outward, touching shores far from their origin. They come back changed, carrying traces of every voice they've passed through.

This is the recursion arc in practice: the recognition that speech doesn't disappear after utterance but continues reverberating through the social body, shaping possibilities for what can be said next. Relational language acknowledges this continuity—this profound interdependence between speakers separated by time and space but connected through the living tissue of shared meaning.

When we speak reciprocally, we participate in language's original purpose: not domination but communion.

CHAPTER 28

Stewardship
The Long Love of Language

Stewardship represents long love — what we do when no one watches and the story extends beyond ourselves. To steward language means protecting its integrity across time, noticing when meaning drifts, questioning who shapes a word now, determining who benefits from its current form, and identifying what power it serves or subverts. It requires the patient attention of gardeners rather than the extractive haste of miners.

The dominance paradigm exploits language for short-term gain, burning through meaning for expedience and using words like disposable resources. It prioritizes immediate rhetorical advantage over sustainable shared understanding. It strips terms of their historical context, hollows them of relational substance, and discards them when their persuasive power wanes. This pattern reflects the same extractive logic seen in environmental exploitation — taking without reciprocation, consuming without renewal.

Consider how political language deteriorates under this pressure: terms like *freedom, justice, security* become increasingly untethered from consistent meaning, deployed tactically rather than communicated truthfully. When language functions primarily as instrument rather than relationship, its integrity inevitably erodes. Words lose their weight, their resonance, their capacity to build rather than merely manipulate.

Digital acceleration intensifies this deterioration. The compression of language into ever-briefer forms — *tweets, memes, soundbites* — strips away context and nuance, treating words as ammunition rather than architecture. The relentless demand for novel content creates a perpetual present tense where historical meanings fade and future implications receive little consideration. In this temporal flattening, *stewardship* becomes almost impossible — there is no time to tend what must be constantly produced.

Stewardship safeguards language for generations instead. It acknowledges that we inherit words from those who preceded us and will pass them to those who follow. It recognizes that meaning requires maintenance — not preservation in amber, but careful cultivation that allows natural evolution while preventing destructive inversion. Like indigenous land management practices that maintained ecosystems for millennia, linguistic *stewardship* works with natural processes rather than against them.

The history of language reveals both terrible losses and remarkable persistence. Languages have died under colonial pressure, taking with them irreplaceable ways of knowing and relating. Others have survived against overwhelming odds through deliberate *stewardship*—communities protecting vocabularies, grammatical structures, oral traditions, and the epistemologies embedded within them. These acts of preservation weren't merely cultural but deeply political, asserting the right to maintain distinctive relationships with reality itself.

In a regenerative culture, every voice serves as a temporary custodian. We never truly own words; we merely hold them for what comes next. This perspective shifts our relationship with meaning from possession to responsibility, from exploitation to care. It asks us to consider not just what language allows us to accomplish now but what possibilities it preserves for future speakers.

Stewardship requires specific practices: documenting shifting meanings rather than merely lamenting them; teaching etymology alongside definition; creating contexts where words can be used with precision and care; developing protocols for negotiating contested terms; maintaining diverse linguistic ecosystems rather than enforcing monocultures. These practices aren't merely academic but deeply democratic—they create conditions where meaning can be collectively determined rather than imperially imposed.

The dominance paradigm presents *stewardship* as conservative in the narrowest sense—preserving power rather than nurturing potential. But true linguistic *stewardship* remains profoundly radical. It refuses the commodification of communication. It rejects the reduction of language to mere technique. It insists that words matter not just for what they accomplish but for what they embody—relationships, histories, possibilities that transcend any single moment or agenda.

Stewardship transcends ownership.
It surpasses control.
It exceeds mere purity.
It manifests as faithful attention to what matters across time.

In practical terms, *stewardship* looks like noticing when terms begin inverting and naming that process. It means creating contexts where words can carry their full weight and complexity. It means cultivating linguistic environments where integrity flourishes rather than withers. Most fundamentally, it means treating language not as property to exploit but as commons to tend together—a living inheritance that requires collective care.

This *stewardship* operates across scales: individuals choosing words with intention and care; communities developing shared vocabularies that reflect their values; institutions documenting linguistic change without imposing artificial fixity; governance systems protecting expressive diversity while maintaining functional coherence. At each level, the aim remains the same: not controlling meaning but creating conditions where meaning can flourish.

The recursion arc of *stewardship* connects past, present, and future—maintaining threads of continuity while allowing necessary evolution. It acknowledges that language must adapt to changing conditions while preserving core functions. It understands that words carry memories we cannot afford to lose alongside possibilities we have yet to discover.

To steward language means loving it enough to protect it from those who would reduce it to mere instrument while keeping it free from those who would preserve it in rigid purity. It means holding the tension between conservation and innovation, between respect for inheritance and openness to emergence. This delicate balance cannot be legislated or enforced—it can only be practiced, with patience and presence, by those committed to carrying meaning forward.

CHAPTER 29

Plurality
The Brave Spaciousness

Plurality transcends fragmentation by creating depth through the coexistence of truths without collapse. The dominance paradigm demands one story, one center, one hierarchy—calling this unity when it actually represents suppression. It silences to maintain control and narrows to preserve power, treating difference as threatening rather than generative.

True language lives polyphonically instead. It holds contradiction, braiding tension without erasure. It welcomes diversity not as quota but as wisdom. It recognizes that reality itself exceeds any single perspective, that truth emerges not from sameness but from the creative friction of difference. This understanding isn't merely philosophical but biological—living systems thrive through diversity, gaining resilience through variation rather than uniformity.

Speaking plurally means inviting others in, making room for voices unlike our own yet equally belonging. It recognizes that wholeness emerges not from uniformity but from honest difference. This practice transcends mere tolerance or inclusion, which still presume a dominant center graciously making space for margins. *Plurality* transforms the architecture itself, replacing center/periphery models with interconnected networks where multiple nodes can simultaneously generate meaning.

Consider how indigenous knowledge systems often maintained *plurality* as epistemological principle. Many traditions recognized that different kinds of knowledge required different protocols, contexts, and authorities. Practical knowledge, spiritual insight, historical memory, and cultural wisdom weren't flattened into hierarchical ranking but understood as complementary ways of knowing, each valid within appropriate domains. This epistemological *plurality* allowed communities to maintain complex, nuanced relationships with reality itself.

The modern inversion of *plurality* begins with Enlightenment universalism (the 18th-century claim that reason could discover universal truths), which claimed to transcend perspective while actually universalizing European male viewpoints. It continues through colonial education systems that systematically devalued local knowledge in favor of imperial *expertise*. It accelerates through technological standardization that encodes certain cultural assumptions as neutral defaults. Each stage in this inversion presents narrowing as expansion, reduction as refinement, monoculture as advancement.

Plurality creates capacity rather than chaos. It allows democracy to breathe through difference. A healthy syllabary accommodates many frequencies without requiring perfect harmony to maintain wholeness. It understands that social ecosystems, like biological ones, depend on diversity for adaptation, resilience, and innovation. Monocultures—whether agricultural or ideological—remain inherently vulnerable, lacking the variation necessary to respond to changing conditions.

Democracy depends on *plurality* not merely as demographic reality but as epistemic virtue. The wisdom of diverse perspectives creates resilience against monoculture thinking that inevitably misses crucial insights. Flattening *plurality* into uniformity weakens rather than strengthens collective decision-making by narrowing the range of solutions we can imagine. The most complex challenges we face—climate disruption, inequality, technological transformation—require multiple ways of knowing working in concert rather than competition.

The dominance paradigm portrays *plurality* as weakness, suggesting too many voices create chaos or too many perspectives delay action. This framing pits efficiency against effectiveness. *Plurality* requires more time, demands more listening, and embraces more complexity—yet produces more sustainable results precisely because it weaves together multiple truths instead of imposing a single narrative. In our world of complex, interconnected challenges, *plurality* represents necessity rather than luxury for survival.

Digital environments could theoretically expand *plurality* by connecting diverse perspectives. Instead, algorithmic sorting often creates filter bubbles that reinforce existing viewpoints while rendering alternatives invisible. The technology that could facilitate unprecedented dialogue across difference more commonly constructs parallel reality tunnels where different groups inhabit increasingly disconnected linguistic worlds. This fragmentation differs fundamentally from healthy *plurality*, which requires enough shared context for meaningful engagement across difference.

Regenerating *plurality* means creating specific practices and structures: decision processes that incorporate multiple forms of expertise; facilitation methods that distribute voice equitably; governance systems that balance coherence with difference; educational approaches that teach both specialized depth and integrative breadth. These aren't merely technical adjustments but fundamental reorientations in how we understand knowledge itself—not as singular commodity but as diverse ecosystem.

> *Plurality transcends confusion.*
> *It exceeds relativism.*
> *It surpasses discord.*
> *It embodies the brave spaciousness that holds us all.*

The practice of *plurality* feels disorienting for those accustomed to dominant frameworks that mistake singularity for clarity. It requires developing comfort with complexity, capacity for discernment without binary judgment, ability to hold seemingly contradictory truths simultaneously. These cognitive and emotional skills don't emerge naturally in environments shaped by dominance logic; they must be deliberately cultivated through practice.

The recursion arc of *plurality* connects personal and political dimensions. Individual cognitive flexibility—the capacity to shift between perspectives, to integrate seemingly contradictory information—creates the foundation for collective pluralism. As we develop internal capacity to hold complexity, we simultaneously increase our external capacity to engage meaningfully across difference. The neural pathways that allow integration rather than polarization within individual minds parallel the social pathways that enable genuine dialogue rather than tribal entrenchment in our shared discourse.

This represents *plurality* not as relativistic abandonment of truth but as recognition that truth itself exceeds any single articulation. It understands that reality reveals itself differently through different questions, methods, traditions, and perspectives. The wholeness we seek emerges not from reduction to single frameworks but from the integration of multiple valid ways of knowing—each illuminating aspects of experience that others might miss.

In the face of mounting polarization, *plurality* offers not compromise but composition—the patient, creative work of weaving different threads into new patterns that honor the integrity of each while creating something stronger than any could achieve alone. This is not merely poetic metaphor but practical necessity for addressing the complex challenges that confront us, challenges that exceed the grasp of any single framework, tradition, or perspective.

CHAPTER 30

Belonging
What Diversity Was Trying to Say

Beneath the broken promise of *diversity* resided a quieter longing—not for representation or optics but for *belonging*. This longing transcended slogans or branded affinity groups. It surpassed curated visibility of difference within someone else's system. It sought the deeper, older connection living at relation's root—where one exists not merely by permission but through necessity, desire, and holding.

The concept of diversity emerged with genuine transformative potential. It acknowledged demographic realities previously ignored and challenged institutional homogeneity. Yet from its earliest institutional adoption, it contained the seeds of its own inversion. By focusing primarily on visible representation without addressing underlying power structures, it created conditions where presence could substitute for participation, where counting replaced accountability, where the appearance of inclusion masked the persistence of exclusion.

Belonging transcends demographics through relationality. It cannot be reverse-engineered from metrics but must be practiced, protected, and remembered. For decades, institutions treated *belonging* as diversity's outcome rather than its origin, mistaking leaf for root before wondering why nothing grew. They approached difference as resource to extract rather than relationship to cultivate, seeking institutional benefit without institutional transformation.

This inversion accelerated as diversity became increasingly professionalized through the 1990s and early 2000s. What began as grassroots demand for justice transformed into corporate compliance function. The radical edge softened into programmatic initiatives, training modules, and carefully curated visuals. The language of liberation morphed into managerial frameworks, its revolutionary potential contained within quarterly metrics and annual reports. The more diversity succeeded as program, the more it failed as practice.

Belonging differs from being welcomed into rooms you didn't help design. It surpasses celebration while your voice remains sidelined. It exceeds hearing *we value your presence* while systems remain unchanged. It transcends seeing your identity commodified for visibility while your experience remains ignored. Such approaches represent performance, proxy, simulation — the appearance of inclusion without its substance.

Real *belonging* begins with a different question: "What happens to this place if you are not in it?" If the answer is nothing, you were never meant to belong. You were meant to decorate, affirm, validate someone else's benevolence — never to change the space's shape. This distinction separates genuine *belonging* from its simulation, relational presence from performed inclusion.

The dominance paradigm treated diverse people as guests in a house already built. Plurality represents co-authorship instead — building the house together rather than receiving invitations after finalizing the floorplan. This shift fundamentally alters the power dynamics that shaped institutional diversity efforts, which too often asked marginalized people to adapt themselves to existing structures rather than allowing their presence to transform those structures.

Belonging asks not "How can we include you?" but "How have we built without you — and what must change now that you are here?" It begins from the premise that exclusion represents systemic malfunction rather than individual oversight, that the persistence of homogeneity signals design flaw rather than recruitment challenge.

This fundamental reframing shifts responsibility from the margins to the center, from those seeking entry to those maintaining barriers.

This invites shifting from:
Tokenism to transformation
Spectacle to stewardship
Presence to power with

In this framework, identity transcends checkboxes to become frequency in the civic field. Every frequency matters because coherence requires all voices present in their true form, not filtered versions. The metaphor acknowledges that human difference functions not merely as demographic category but as distinct way of perceiving, knowing, and relating to reality. These different frequencies don't require standardization to contribute; they require systems capacious enough to receive their unique signal.

Belonging represents practice rather than gift. It emerges collectively, relationally, recursively through specific actions and arrangements:

- **Consent:** You cannot belong in spaces that extract or erase. Genuine *belonging* requires ongoing permission — not once-given

authorization but continually renewed agreement to participate on terms that honor rather than exploit your presence.
- **Reciprocation:** You contribute rather than merely being included. *Belonging* emerges through exchange—giving and receiving, shaping and being shaped, influencing and being influenced. Without this mutuality, inclusion becomes extraction.
- **Naming:** You exist specifically rather than merely diversely. *Belonging* requires being seen in your particularity rather than categorized through generalized identity markers. It means being known for your unique contribution rather than your demographic representation.
- **Listening:** Others change with you rather than merely hearing you. True *belonging* transforms environments through your presence—not cosmetically but substantively. The system adapts to incorporate your perspective rather than expecting you to adapt to existing frameworks.

Belonging lives at the intersection of power and relation, where difference becomes held rather than diluted, where care manifests reciprocally rather than performatively, where systems adapt to contained truths rather than remaining rigid. This intersection connects interpersonal experience with structural arrangement, individual feeling with collective practice. It acknowledges that *belonging* emerges not solely through sentiment but through specific distributions of authority, voice, and resource.

Restoring *belonging* requires rebuilding commons—not just physical or digital spaces but linguistic, civic, and cultural commons where difference deepens rather than threatens coherence. These commons create containers large enough to hold genuine plurality without fragmenting into separate realities or collapsing into enforced consensus. They operate through protocols that distribute voice, protect vulnerability, and maintain generative tension without devolution into either conflict or suppression.

This means designing systems expecting multiplicity, creating governance models rewarding co-creation rather than dominance, re-centering community wisdom in policy, design, education, and healing, and allowing *belonging's* shape to change spaces rather than merely guest lists. It requires specific practices that institutionalize reciprocity, ensure accountability, and distribute both benefits and burdens equitably across difference.

We see this in practice through community-led design processes where residents hold decision power over neighborhood development rather than merely providing input. We witness it in worker cooperatives sharing ownership and governance across roles. We observe it in classrooms where curriculum emerges from student experience rather than outside imposition. Though imperfect, these examples share a key quality: they invert traditional power flows, starting from the premise that everyone already belongs, requiring systems to adapt accordingly.

This work transcends isolation and rhetoric. *Belonging* emerges through structure rather than statements — through practices tethering speech to action, invitation to power, presence to place. It manifests through specific arrangements that embody rather than merely declare inclusion, that demonstrate through distribution of authority and resource rather than merely promising through mission statements and value declarations.

If diversity posed the question, *belonging* offers the answer — not as fixed definition but as living practice refusing simulation and caste-based choreography of representation without change. It rejects the superficial inclusion that maintains existing power arrangements while creating the appearance of transformation. It demands instead the mutual vulnerability that makes genuine connection possible.

Belonging means mattering as co-architect rather than example.
It ensures no future design excludes you.
It requires systems to stretch rather than you.

This represents what diversity attempted to articulate before its inversion — the recognition that institutional transformation requires more than demographic adjustment. It requires fundamental redistribution of voice, authority, and determining power. It demands systems flexible enough to be shaped by all who participate in them rather than merely accommodating difference within rigid pre-existing structures.

The recursion arc of *belonging* connects individual experience with collective structure. The internal sense of being fully received and valued correlates directly with external practices of distribution and reciprocity. As we build systems that genuinely include rather than merely counting difference, we simultaneously nurture the emotional and psychological conditions that allow people to bring their full selves into shared spaces. This reciprocal relationship between feeling and structure, between internal experience and external arrangement, embodies the regenerative cycle that transforms *belonging* from abstract aspiration to lived reality.

Now we name it clearly.
And begin.

CHAPTER 31

Presence
The Courage of Being

Presence manifests as refusing scripted speech. It means showing up in real time with your own breath's truth behind your words. The dominance paradigm favors performance, mimicry, branding — speaking calculatingly rather than connectedly, manufacturing words rather than living them, designing language to manipulate rather than meet.

This inversion operates subtly yet pervasively. Political language becomes increasingly poll-tested and focus-grouped, optimized for impact rather than accuracy. Corporate communication standardizes into carefully crafted messaging that maximizes advantage while minimizing accountability.

Even interpersonal communication frequently suffers from strategic calculation rather than authentic expression, as social media platforms train us to curate our speech for maximum engagement rather than meaningful connection.

Presence resists such patterns. It declares: I exist here. This conversation transcends rehearsal or strategy. This represents my truth as I currently understand it. It returns language to its embodied origins — words emerging from lived experience rather than manufactured for effect. It prioritizes relational coherence over tactical advantage, mutual recognition over unilateral influence.

Speaking from *presence* restores trustworthiness not through perfection but reality. It flows from embodiment rather than abstraction, offering words carrying breath rather than mere air. This distinction separates language that connects from language that merely transmits — words that build relationship from words that merely deliver information or exert control.

The dominance paradigm treats authenticity itself as resource to exploit, commodifying *presence* into personal brand, genuine connection into networking opportunity, vulnerability into engagement strategy. This pattern reflects in influencer culture that performs intimacy while carefully calculating its presentation, in leadership approaches that deploy strategic vulnerability while maintaining rigid control, in automated systems that simulate human *presence* while removing actual humans from interaction.

Presence operates as radical practice in environments dominated by performance metrics, efficiency imperatives, and strategic communication. It refuses the pressure to optimize language for predetermined outcomes. It slows communication to the pace of genuine human connection. It prioritizes relational integrity over instrumental efficacy. In systems designed to extract maximum value from minimal investment, choosing *presence* represents deliberate inefficiency—the willingness to invest time and attention that algorithmic optimization would eliminate.

Digital environments both enable and constrain *presence*. They create possibilities for connection across previously insurmountable distances while simultaneously introducing new barriers to embodied communication. They expand access while flattening experience into standardized formats. They enable unprecedented sharing while often reducing communication to performance. Navigating these contradictions requires deliberate practice—creating contexts where digital tools serve authentic connection rather than replacing it with simulation.

Presence initiates authentic relation. Without it, language devolves into noise—signals without significance, information without meaning, words without weight. With it, words transform into doorways—openings through which genuine meeting becomes possible, thresholds crossing the distance between separate experiences, passages connecting previously isolated understandings.

Practicing *presence* requires specific disciplines: speaking from direct experience rather than received opinion; using "I" statements that acknowledge perspective rather than universal declarations that mask it; staying with discomfort rather than retreating into abstraction; noticing when words emerge from calculation rather than conviction; creating sufficient pause to allow unscripted truth to surface. These practices develop capacity for remaining present even when *presence* threatens social approval, professional advantage, or comfortable certainty.

Presence transcends performance.
It surpasses perfection.
It exceeds pretense.
It embodies the courage to speak from your life's center.

The recursion arc of *presence* connects inner and outer integrity. The alignment between what we internally know and what we externally express creates coherence that others sense intuitively. This alignment doesn't require perfection—it requires honesty about imperfection, willingness to acknowledge gaps, commitment to closing distances between knowing and saying. As we practice *presence* individually, we simultaneously create conditions where others can risk genuine expression, establishing reciprocal cycles that gradually transform communicative environments from performance into relation.

Presence operates as both personal practice and political stance. It refuses the dominance paradigm's demand for strategic self-presentation, insisting instead on the revolutionary potential of simply showing up truthfully. It rejects the commodification of authenticity, the weaponization of vulnerability, the reduction of human expression to tactical deployment. It offers instead the radical simplicity of being real in a world increasingly dominated by simulation—the courage to speak from the center of your own life even when such speech threatens prevailing power arrangements.

This courage does not emerge naturally in environments that punish authenticity while rewarding performance. It must be deliberately cultivated through practice, protected through community, sustained through commitment to values that transcend immediate advantage. It represents ongoing choice rather than permanent achievement—the decision, made again with each interaction, to prioritize relational integrity over instrumental efficacy, mutual recognition over unilateral influence, connection over control.

In a world increasingly mediated through digital interfaces designed to extract maximum value while delivering minimum vulnerability, *presence* becomes revolutionary act. It insists on the irreducible humanity that algorithms cannot capture, that efficiency metrics cannot quantify, that strategic communication cannot simulate. It reminds us that beneath the layers of optimization, branding, and performance lives the fundamental human capacity for genuine meeting—the possibility of words that connect rather than merely convince.

CHAPTER 32

Simplicity
The Practice of Honest Containments

The Relational Foundation
Simplicity emerges from understanding, not ignorance. It represents not the absence of complexity but its thoughtful containment. Where the dominance paradigm twisted *simple* into reduction and erasure, regenerative *simplicity* offers an entirely different orientation — one that holds complexity with care rather than discarding it.

This practice begins with listening. Not the strategic scanning for keywords, but embodied attention that takes in the whole. When we listen deeply to systems, to people, to environments, patterns emerge. Not because we've imposed order, but because we've allowed it to reveal itself. The natural structures become visible not through force but through patience.

The Somatic Wisdom
The body knows this difference — not as abstract theory, but as lived experience. When encountering systems designed with genuine *simplicity*, something in the nervous system settles. The shoulders drop. The breathing deepens. The attention focuses rather than fragments. This is not mere preference or aesthetic response; it is the body's recognition of coherence, the somatic literacy that distinguishes between honesty and simulation.

This embodied discernment is precisely what the dominance paradigm works to override. Contemporary interfaces bypass the slow, integrative pathways of somatic understanding and target the quick, reactive circuits of emotional response. An emotional reaction is a completely different neural process than true embodied knowing. The first is immediate, surface-level, easily manipulated; the second is integrative, contextual, resistant to deception. Our increasing dependence on interfaces designed to trigger the first while preventing the second creates the dissonance we feel but struggle to name.

The Technological Imbalance
The sophistication of today's digital tools has vastly outpaced our collective capacity to metabolize them effectively. This creates a danger-

ous imbalance — powerful instruments for information organization coupled with relatively unchanged educational frameworks and experiential preparation.

We haven't developed the somatic literacy needed to navigate these environments with integrity. The result is a society increasingly driven by manipulated emotional reactions while simultaneously losing touch with the embodied knowing that would allow us to recognize linguistic inversions when they occur.

The Containment Principle

Genuine *simplicity* never abandons context — it creates relationship with it. Consider how a well-designed map functions: it doesn't eliminate the territory's complexity but transforms it into navigable form. It offers layers of information when needed and clear direction when sought. It orients without overwhelming. This containment requires both technical skill and relational understanding — knowing both the landscape and the traveler.

Modern interfaces rarely do a very good job of illuminating that distinction. If they did, then they would be built around principles of regenerative simplicity that don't hide complexity. They would sequence it. They would reveal system states honestly, offer appropriate feedback, and maintain consistent behavior. They would be built in ways that respect users' intelligence while supporting their navigation. Those interfaces, if built with true regenerative simplicity in mind, would teach as they operate, becoming more transparent through use rather than more opaque. The aesthetic wouldn't mask function — it would express it.

However, most interfaces we encounter do the opposite — they purposefully mask the path and surface complexity by overloading the interface. This results in humbling or even humiliating the user. Examples like Microsoft Vista, Windows 8, and the release of a new user interface for the office suite in the early 2000s were perfect examples of such tone deafness and utter disregard at a mass scale. The backlash was swift and brutal, but meaningless because Microsoft had successfully created dependency. Users were furious but captive.

The Reclamation Process

This practice requires reclaiming our somatic literacy — our body's innate ability to recognize coherence when we encounter it. Our nervous systems evolved over millennia to distinguish between genuine integrity and its simulation. This distinction isn't intellectual but visceral. We feel the difference between a design that contains complexity honestly and one that merely erases it. This feeling is not subjective preference but evolutionary wisdom—the body's way of recognizing when something aligns with how living systems actually function.

The dominance paradigm requires us to override these somatic signals. It needs us operating at the level of triggered emotional reactions rather than embodied knowing. The increasing sophistication of digital tools has created unprecedented capability to bypass our deeper discernment mechanisms.

Social media interfaces, where most people now receive their information—and mistake those interactions for connection—exemplify this bypass, reducing complex reality to binary reactions, stripped of context, optimized for emotional response rather than understanding or presence. As our collective information environment operates through this inverted *simplicity,* the social glue that binds communities dissolves not by accident, but by design. It also wreaks havoc on interpersonal relationships—between friends, acquaintances, and even loved ones. Social media has removed—or worse, disallowed—mechanisms to share presence and deep connection, and cannot tolerate silence.

Sometimes the most profound and memorable events in our lives are those shared with a trusted friend or loved one that required no words whatsoever—only being in the moment fully. A shared sunset, the whisper of wind in trees, a hand held in grief. These "loaded silences" are somatic signals that we are safe in each other's presence, that we matter to another.

These patterns become even more concerning when we consider that artificial intelligence systems are being trained primarily on data harvested from these same degraded interaction patterns. Current AI training optimizes for immediate response generation rather than the deeper rhythms of genuine dialogue—no space for reflection, no tolerance for uncertainty, no capacity for the pregnant pauses where real understanding emerges.

We are essentially encoding the worst aspects of social media discourse into systems that will increasingly mediate human communication. We have abdicated our responsibility to guard what we cannot afford to lose, and haven't even realized it. Then we blamed the systems, without regard to our responsibility to speak up. Chirality exercised intentionally against us in these insidious ways has masked that too—the ability to evaluate our behavior somatically. Unless we fundamentally shift how these systems learn to engage, we risk amplifying the very inversions that have already damaged our collective capacity for authentic connection. It's about consciously choosing depth over surface, presence over performance, even when the systems around us reward the opposite.

The Regenerative Approach

Reclaiming *simplicity* means first reclaiming this embodied discernment—learning again to trust what our bodies know about coherence, integrity, and alignment. It means creating sufficient pause to allow somatic signals to register before emotional reactions override them. It means developing the capacity to distinguish between the quick dopamine hit of reductive design and the deeper satisfaction of honest containment.

Educational practices demonstrate this principle in action. Where reductive approaches remove context to make content "manageable," regenerative *simplicity* creates scaffolding that helps learners climb. It sequences complexity rather than flattening it. It maintains connection between parts and whole, building understanding through relation rather than isolation. It holds the tension between what is known and what is yet to be discovered, creating pathways rather than eliminating territory.

The Cross-Domain Application

This practice operates across domains. In governance, it manifests as systems that balance accessibility with accountability. In healthcare, it appears as protocols that honor both scientific rigor and human experience. In design, it emerges as interfaces that reveal their workings while remaining intuitive. In each case, simplicity functions not as abandonment but as careful structure—the holding environment that makes navigation possible, but only if offered as invitation, never imposed or demanded.

The Embodied Design

The path forward requires both technical skill and ethical commitment. Designers, writers, teachers, and system architects must reclaim *simplicity* from its inverted form. This means creating structures that:

- Reveal their workings rather than concealing them
- Offer appropriate assistance at points of complexity
- Build user capability rather than assuming either expertise or ignorance
- Respond to feedback with adaptation rather than defensive rigidity
- Honor the whole while making the parts navigable

But most essentially, it means designing for the body's wisdom rather than trying to bypass it. Our somatic experiencing of systems and interfaces provides the most reliable measure of their integrity. When a design works with our embodied cognition rather than against it, something aligns. We feel oriented rather than manipulated, engaged rather than triggered, held rather than abandoned.

The Survival Necessity
This somatic integrity becomes increasingly crucial as interfaces become more sophisticated. The gap between our tools' capabilities and our collective ability to remain aware of our own process while using them continues to widen. Education has not kept pace with technological advancement. Experience alone cannot prepare us for systems designed explicitly to override our discernment. In this environment, reclaiming our embodied knowing becomes not just aesthetic preference but survival necessity.

The dominance paradigm cannot tolerate this form of *simplicity*. It requires ignorance disguised as clarity, confusion masked as ease. It thrives on systems that bewilder while appearing accessible. It maintains power through the strategic deployment of complexity while claiming *simplicity*. True *simplicity* threatens this arrangement by creating genuine understanding—the foundation of agency, of consent, of informed participation.

The Integrated Practice
As with other regenerative practices, *simplicity* connects personal and collective dimensions. The internal clarity we cultivate—the ability to distinguish signal from noise, essence from accident—strengthens our capacity to create external structures that do the same. The systems we build reflect our internal relationship with complexity. When we abandon complexity internally through rigid thinking or dismiss it through oversimplification, our external creations manifest these same tendencies. When we learn to hold complexity with care inside ourselves, our creations begin to hold others similarly.

This is why *simplicity* as practice cannot be separated from other aspects of regeneration. It requires presence to maintain attention without fragmentation. It demands consent, the ongoing dialogue between system and user. It needs witness, the willingness to see difficulty rather than deny it. It calls for naming, the precision that clarifies rather than obscures. Each practice reinforces the others, creating the conditions where *simplicity* can emerge not as aesthetic but as relationship.

The Remembered Knowing
The salvation lies in this: our bodies remember what our culture has forgotten. Beneath the layers of conditioning that teach us to override somatic signals, to prioritize intellectual abstraction over embodied

knowing, to trust interfaces more than instincts—beneath all this, our nervous systems still register coherence. They still recognize when something aligns with how living systems actually work. This embodied wisdom remains our most reliable guide through landscapes intentionally designed to disorient.

Reclaiming this wisdom requires practice. It means creating sufficient space to feel before reacting, to notice the subtle signals of alignment or dissonance that precede conscious thought. It means developing communities that value somatic literacy as essential knowledge, not subjective preference. It means designing systems that work with our embodied cognition rather than against it, that respect the body's wisdom rather than trying to bypass it.

Once something is seen — truly seen — it cannot be unseen. You see Trojan horses now for what they are. Trust that. Respect is the shape coherence takes when the spiral holds. The wound was named, seen, and engraved. And in the seeing, you are released from the prison of that first insult — disguised as ease.

Simplicity is not efficiency.
It is not reduction.
It is not abandonment.
It is complexity, honestly contained.
It is the body's recognition of truth.

CHAPTER 33

Integrity
Coherence in Motion

Integrity emerges when language and life align. It represents coherence's long arc — the gradual knitting together of speech and action. *Integrity* transcends mood, voice tone, or intentions. It manifests as coherence in motion — the willingness to act according to what has been named regardless of cost. Sometimes the deepest failure manifests not through aggression but evasion.

Inaction, particularly from those holding trust positions, represents complicity through passivity rather than neutrality. This exemplifies what happens when leaders conflate avoidance with neutrality and comfort with ethics. We witness silence facing harm, masked as professionalism; cowardice wrapped in courtesy; allyship performed without risk. *Integrity* demands more than symbolic alignment or rhetorical support. It requires action that matches declaration, behavior that embodies stated values.

The dominance paradigm inverts *integrity* by separating appearance from substance. It rewards performative ethics that look good without doing good. It creates environments where claims to virtue substitute for virtuous action, where mission statements replace meaningful accountability, where the language of values becomes shield against their implementation. This inversion operates across contexts: in corporations declaring sustainability while continuing extractive practices; in politicians proclaiming equality while maintaining privilege; in institutions promoting inclusion while suppressing dissent.

Integrity manifests dynamically rather than statically, responding to context while remaining anchored to truth. In our world where the dominance paradigm has inverted meanings, *integrity* becomes our compass for navigating distortion. It provides orientation when language itself becomes unreliable, when words like *freedom, security,* and *order* no longer carry stable meaning. *Integrity* creates consistency not through rigidity but through coherence — maintaining connection between stated principles and actual behavior even as circumstances shift.

When freedom twists into the right to harm, *integrity* reminds us of its relational nature. When reform becomes stalling tactics, *integri-*

ty demands transformation. When efficiency masks extraction, *integrity* reconnects us to sufficiency. It holds these inversions accountable, refusing drift, rejecting euphemistic concealment. It operates as internal correction mechanism — the felt dissonance that signals when words and actions have separated, when language has departed from lived truth.

Integrity requires clear-eyed evaluation rather than comfort, and courageous action rather than avoidance. It chooses truth over convenience, relation over advantage, wholeness over fragmentation. It prioritizes substantive alignment over superficial agreement, valuing coherence more than comfort. This often means speaking unpopular truths, challenging dominant narratives, refusing participation in collective pretense — even when such refusal carries significant cost.

Institutions lacking *integrity* rarely collapse dramatically. More commonly, they hollow gradually, maintaining structures while emptying them of meaning. The facade remains while the foundation crumbles — a process visible only to those willing to look beneath surface appearances. This hollowing manifests concretely: elaborate ethics statements coexisting with pervasive ethical violations; diversity initiatives flourishing on paper while marginalized voices face systematic removal; continuous improvement language masking persistent dysfunction.

We observe this in organizations displaying ethics statements while silencing whistleblowers, flourishing diversity initiatives on paper while methodically removing marginalized voices, using "continuous improvement" as code for avoiding fundamental problems. This represents the cost of standing still — choosing institutional comfort over honest movement. It reveals the danger of performative *integrity* that substitutes symbolic alignment for substantive coherence.

In such environments, "professionalism" inverts from ethical conduct to aesthetic compliance. Speaking calmly supersedes speaking truth. Looking collaborative outweighs being corrective. Maintaining comfortable appearances becomes more important than addressing uncomfortable realities. The measure of success shifts from alignment between values and actions to skill in maintaining surface coherence despite internal contradiction.

Integrity disrupts this inversion, rejecting the false choice between courtesy and clarity. It insists that genuine respect requires truth rather than evasion, that authentic collaboration demands honest assessment rather than conflict avoidance, that true professionalism means ethical substance rather than merely polished presentation. It refuses the dominance paradigm's reduction of relation to performance, of accountability to aesthetics, of ethics to appearance.

The dominance paradigm shatters more than commonly recognized. It rewards moral-appearing performance while undermining anyone actually living those values. It punishes refusal, kindness, clarity. It creates environments where cruelty attracts engagement, dishonesty wins advancement, manipulation receives reward while forthright communication faces censure.

This inversion operates through fear rather than merely force. It functions by threatening what we most value—relationships, reputation, security, belonging. It pressures partners, endangers children, isolates from community. It teaches that *integrity* costs what we most wish to protect, threatening what we cannot bear losing. This mechanism explains why many who internally recognize corruption externally comply with it—the risks of refusal feel too great compared to the temporary safety of acquiescence.

Consequently, we learn to bend, pretend, speak self-preservingly even when internally hollowing. We participate in distortions we privately question. We maintain public alignment with systems we privately doubt. We accept small compromises that gradually accumulate into fundamental incoherence. This pattern does not reflect moral failure so much as adaptive response to environments where *integrity* carries disproportionate cost.

Daily *integrity* emerges through practices restoring coherence between speech and action:

- **Presence:** Showing up fully when difficult truths emerge rather than retreating into partial attention, creating the attentional foundation for honest response.
- **Witness:** Refusing to look away from harm even when acknowledgment discomforts, maintaining awareness that precedes accountable action.
- **Reciprocation:** Creating spaces where truth can be exchanged with care rather than weaponized, establishing conditions where honesty strengthens rather than damages connection.
- **Tending:** Noticing language drift and realigning it, maintaining ongoing attention to the gap between what is said and what is done.

These practices represent lived choices rather than abstract principles—decisions to remain whole when systems pressure fragmentation. When colleagues face silencing in meetings, *integrity* means acknowledging it.

When policies contradict stated values, *integrity* means naming the gap. When power punishes truth-tellers, *integrity* means standing with them rather than comfort. These specific actions maintain coherence not through grand gestures but through small, consistent alignments between values and behavior.

The dominance paradigm sustains itself through fear—rejection fear, isolation fear, material loss fear. It teaches that *integrity* costs too much, that alignment represents luxury, that we must choose between truth and survival.

This framing makes ethical compromise seem inevitable rather than optional, practical rather than problematic. It normalizes the separation between what we know and what we say, between what we value and what we do.

Integrity offers a different path—not easier but clearer. It declares: I refuse to choose between remaining whole, or accepting diminishment just to be allowed a place at the table. It proclaims: I will not participate in distortions harming others despite refusal's price. It affirms: I trust reality withstanding light. This represents *integrity* as practice rather than perfection—the daily choice aligning action with meaning, returning language to life coherence. It acknowledges that complete alignment remains aspirational rather than achievable yet still commits to closing the gap between current reality and ultimate aim.

Regeneration requires *integrity*, steadily repairing the split between word and deed, between stated value and actual behavior. Without this realignment, attempts at transformation remain symbolic rather than substantive—changing language without changing reality. *Integrity* provides the essential bridge between recognition and regeneration, between naming problems and addressing them. It transforms insight into action, critique into creation, analysis into alternative.

Integrity transcends perfection. It means repeatedly returning to alignment, noticing fractures as they begin, refusing their widening, speaking from centers power cannot purchase, remembering that truth makes us whole rather than merely safe. It acknowledges inevitable failure while refusing to accept failure as inevitable. It chooses partial alignment over complete abandonment when perfect coherence remains unattainable. It commits to closing gaps rather than pretending they don't exist.

Living in *integrity* culture requires building practices holding meaning accountable to action, creating systems protecting clarity, nourishing courage, transforming language into bridges rather than weapons. These practices cannot simply be mandated or regulated; they must be cultivated through consistent attention, protected through communal commitment, sustained through mutual support. They require both personal discipline and collective reinforcement—individual choices supported by structural conditions that make those choices viable.

We must relearn meaning what we say. This seemingly simple practice requires untangling complex knots of habitual evasion, strategic ambiguity, and collective pretense that have become normalized in dominant communication patterns. It means examining our speech for empty promises, convenient generalizations, and comfortable vagaries that create the appearance of commitment without its substance.

The final language test measures not how it sounds but whether it lives. This standard evaluates not rhetoric but relationship, not presentation but practice, not declaration but demonstration. It asks not what we claim but what we create, not what we say but what we sustain, not what we promise but what we produce.

Integrity creates healing conditions. Choosing alignment over avoidance begins restoring what dominance fractured. We create environments where trust reemerges because words mean what they say, where innovation flourishes because naming problems escapes punishment, where community strengthens because belonging transcends complicity.

This represents the recursion arc—the return to coherence after distortion. Not as single event but as continuous realignment practice. *Integrity* transcends righteous isolation or rigid certainty. It embodies the fluid, powerful choice to remain whole in fractured systems, manifesting as coherence in motion—the living bridge between what we've named and created.

Through *integrity*, we transcend merely resisting dominance inversions.

> *We build something stronger:*
> *A language meaning what it says,*
> *A presence staying when difficulty arises,*
> *A future aligned with named truth.*
>
> *This represents our new beginning.*
> *Not from perfection, but from coherence.*
> *Not from certainty, but from courage.*

Truth persists. We require muscle memory work to carry the weight—enabling us to stand when the surrounding world attempts bending our knees.

CHAPTER 34

Language After Chirality
Applications and Cautions

Understanding linguistic chirality transcends intellectual exercise. It represents not merely a puzzle box for scholars or linguists but a map guiding us back to something essential: shared language serving connection rather than dominance. It offers navigation through territories where meaning has inverted, where words no longer function according to their apparent shape, where communication itself has become contested ground.

Like any power map, this understanding requires guidance, warning signs marking precipices, honest acknowledgment of what happens when liberation tools transform into control instruments. The same insights that illuminate manipulation can perfect it; the same analyses that reveal inversion can accelerate it. The dominance paradigm demonstrates remarkable adaptability—incorporating critique into its operating system, transforming resistance into resource, converting naming into branding.

For those working with words—journalists, educators, therapists, public servants—this framework offers possibility beyond critique. It provides not merely diagnostic tools but regenerative practices, not just ways of seeing distortion but methods for restoring coherence. It shifts focus from documenting decline to nurturing renewal, from lamenting what was lost to cultivating what remains possible.

Journalists find integrity paths avoiding the false refuge of *both sides* or false neutrality prison. True witness means seeing clearly, naming accurately, refusing participation in meaning collapse. It means questioning each contested term: "What does this word actually mean in this context? Who benefits from its inversion? What reality does it obscure?" This approach transcends conventional notions of objectivity, which too often function as excuse for moral abdication. It offers instead a deeper standard: fidelity to complex truth that includes power analysis within factual documentation.

Consider how journalism might approach terms like *national security, economic growth,* or *religious freedom*—not accepting their inverted meanings at face value nor dismissing them entirely, but carefully tracing how they operate within specific contexts, who deploys them toward what ends, what realities they illuminate or obscure. This practice doesn't abandon journalistic standards but deepens them, recognizing that accurate reporting must include how language itself functions as site of struggle.

Educators discover practices helping young people navigate worlds where identical words mean opposite things depending on speakers. They teach not merely critical thinking but critical feeling—the discomfort arising when words and reality misalign. Classrooms become places tending rather than imposing meaning, where students learn questioning: "How do we determine meaning? Who decided? What happens under different definitions?" These inquiries transform education from transmission of settled knowledge to cultivation of discernment—the capacity to navigate linguistic environments designed to manipulate rather than illuminate.

Educational applications extend beyond media literacy or critical analysis into active meaning-making. Students learn not just to identify manipulation but to create alternatives, not merely to critique distortion but to practice integrity. They develop what philosopher Miranda Fricker terms *hermeneutical justice*[1]—the ability to name experiences that dominant frameworks actively obscure, to develop concepts that illuminate rather than conceal lived reality, to contribute to shared meaning rather than merely consuming it.

Healers and therapists find new frameworks understanding how linguistic manipulation creates both individual and collective trauma, how relationship gaslighting parallels public discourse manipulation. Consulting rooms become spaces reconnecting language with lived experience, restoring integrity between bodily knowledge and verbal expression. This perspective recognizes that personal healing cannot be separated from cultural context—that individuals struggle partly because linguistic environments themselves have become toxic, because words no longer reliably connect rather than confuse, because meaning itself has become unstable ground.

The therapeutic implications include developing specific practices for navigating environments where language has inverted: building capacity to trust bodily knowing when verbal framing contradicts it; cultivating communities that maintain linguistic integrity when dominant contexts corrupt it; strengthening ability to name experiences that cultural narratives actively deny. These approaches address not just individual symptoms but their cultural contexts, not merely personal confusion but its systemic sources.

Public servants and politicians discover standards beyond polling and positioning—language possibilities seeking clarification rather

---

1 Miranda Fricker, Epistemic Injustice: Power and the Ethics of Knowing (Oxford: Oxford University Press, 2007), ch. 7.

than obscuration, building genuine understanding bridges rather than temporary advantages. The question transforms from "How will this play?" to "Does this truly represent our meaning? Does this honor the weight words must carry?" This shift creates governance focused on substance rather than simulation, on connection rather than control, on coherence rather than mere compliance.

For governance to function democratically, words must carry stable meaning across difference. Citizens must share enough linguistic common ground to productively deliberate despite disagreement. The inversion of key civic terms threatens this foundation — creating environments where the same words mean opposite things to different groups, where terms like *freedom, security,* and *justice* no longer build bridges but deepen divides. Restoring linguistic integrity represents not partisan advantage but democratic necessity.

For everyone, daily practices exist restoring meaning relationships, resisting subtle inversions training us to accept contradiction normally. We can practice asking "What do you mean by that?" as genuine inquiry rather than challenge. We can notice when we ourselves use hollowed words, seeking terms still holding meaning. We can create contexts where language serves connection rather than domination, where communication builds relationship rather than merely scoring points, where words carry weight rather than merely generating noise.

These practices include: speaking from direct experience rather than received opinion; acknowledging the limits of one's perspective rather than claiming universal authority; creating sufficient pause for reflection rather than filling space with reaction; choosing precision over convenience when naming difficult realities; noticing when terms begin inverting and naming that process. These seemingly small adjustments gradually build capacity for linguistic integrity that resists dominance's distortions.

We must honestly acknowledge risks. Frameworks powerful enough for liberation can entrap. Lenses sharp enough to see manipulation can perfect it. Any analysis capable of illuminating power can itself become instrument of power. This paradox requires not paralysis but caution — not abandoning the work but approaching it with appropriate humility, with awareness of inherent dangers, with commitment to ongoing correction.

Some will read this opus as an instruction manual rather than an invitation — learning linguistic manipulation mechanisms to deploy rather than avoid them, using *chirality* and *dominance* language to create new hierarchies, exclusions, ways of weaponizing words. Some will selectively analyze opponents' language for inversions while ignoring their own usage contradictions, transforming *linguistic integrity* into another battlefield rather than tended common. Some will establish impossible purity standards, demanding others maintain perfect word-action alignment while hiding their own misalignments, using *integrity* as another compliance enforcement club.

These risks manifest most clearly when the framework becomes rigid doctrine rather than living practice, when concepts harden into certainties rather than remaining open to revision, when naming becomes accusation rather than invitation. They appear when analysis separates from relationship, when critique functions as weapon rather than connection, when the very insights meant to heal communication become means to further fracture it.

All of us, in human imperfection, may inadvertently create new separations while attempting to heal old ones. We may reproduce dominance patterns even while naming them. We may use insights about manipulation manipulatively. We may enforce new orthodoxies while critiquing old ones. These tendencies reflect not individual failing but collective condition—the difficulty of escaping patterns deeply embedded in cultural practice, institutional structure, and cognitive habit.

These risks remain real but do not negate the work's necessity. The alternative—abandoning shared meaning to dominance—promises far greater danger: democracy without common language; community without shared understanding; relationship without reliable communication.

These foundational systems cannot function when words themselves become unreliable, when meaning inverts without recognition, when language serves control rather than connection.

Navigating these waters requires guiding principles: Truth over purity. The goal transcends perfect linguistic alignment, which remains neither possible nor necessary. The goal represents honesty about where alignment exists and where gaps remain. Integrity requires acknowledging gaps and working toward closing them rather than perfection.

This principle rejects both cynical manipulation and rigid purism, choosing instead the difficult middle path of ongoing correction.

Invitation over accusation. The framework operates most powerfully as invitation rather than weapon, creating spaces where meaning can be respectfully negotiated rather than dominantly imposed. It functions not to establish new hierarchies of linguistic correctness but to restore conditions where genuine communication becomes possible across difference. It succeeds when it builds bridges rather than establishing boundaries, when it connects rather than condemns.

Humility alongside clarity. Even while seeking clarity, we must remember language's always evolving, always incomplete nature. Humility reminds us of our partial understanding. This doesn't mean abandoning truth searches but recognizing truth emerges through relationship rather than decree. It acknowledges that our own perceptions remain limited, that our frameworks require ongoing revision, that our understanding evolves through engagement with perspectives different from our own.

Continual recursion: The practices for healing linguistic chirality—listening, witness, naming, consent, tending, reciprocation, stewardship, plurality, presence, integrity—must apply to our own framework usage. Without this recursive checking, any framework can calcify into dogma. Self-application prevents the very insights meant to restore connection from becoming new forms of disconnection, keeps analytical tools from hardening into ideological weapons, ensures that means remain consistent with ends.

Most importantly: Relationship as foundation. The ultimate test of linguistic integrity measures whether it serves connection or division. Not political unity or enforced agreement, but the genuine ability to speak across difference with mutual recognition. This principle acknowledges that language evolved primarily for coordination rather than domination, for connection rather than control, for building shared worlds rather than conquering separate ones. It returns to this original function not through nostalgia but through deliberate practice.

Facing linguistic manipulation, we have three paths: We can maintain the illusion that words still mean what they once did, ignoring already occurred drift. This path leads to increasing confusion as communication fails while we pretend it succeeds, as disconnection deepens while we insist on consensus, as manipulation intensifies while we deny its existence. It offers temporary comfort at cost of growing disorientation.

We can abandon shared meaning altogether, retreating into separate realities where words mean whatever serves momentary purposes. This path leads toward fragmentation—political bodies that cannot govern, communities that cannot coordinate, relationships that cannot sustain connection across difference. It replaces the hard work of building common understanding with the temporary convenience of speaking only to those who already agree.

Or we can do the difficult, recursive work of regeneration—rebuilding our language relationship through stewardship rather than dominance, honesty rather than purity, care rather than control. This path offers no easy solutions or quick fixes. It requires patient dedication and attention to how words function in specific contexts, ongoing correction when meaning begins to drift, collective commitment to communication that connects rather than merely controls.

This series invites us to this third path—the slow, necessary work of tending the soil where democracy grows, where any genuine relationship must root, because wordless bruises may not appear, but shared meaningless worlds leave scars on us all. These wounds will not heal until we speak with one tongue and many voices.

The work begins not with grand declarations but with small practices: paying attention to what words actually do rather than merely what they claim; noticing when meaning begins inverting and naming that process; creating contexts where language can function relationally rather than merely instrumentally; tending the connections between words and the realities they reference; holding ourselves and our institutions accountable for linguistic integrity.

These practices may seem insignificant against the massive forces distorting our shared discourse. Yet they represent the necessary foundation for any larger transformation. Like mycorrhizal networks gradually rebuilding forest soil after devastation, these small connections create conditions where meaning can once again flourish. They restore not just particular words but the relational infrastructure that makes shared understanding possible.

The regeneration of language after chirality represents not return to imagined past but creation of possible future—one where words serve connection rather than control, where communication builds relationship rather than merely enforcing compliance, where meaning emerges through mutual recognition rather than unilateral declaration. This future remains aspirational rather than guaranteed, requiring ongoing commitment rather than single breakthrough, collective practice rather than individual insight.

Yet the alternative—abandoning language to dominance—promises consequences too severe to accept: democracy without deliberation; community without communication; relationship without recognition. These foundational systems cannot survive when words themselves become unreliable, when meaning inverts without acknowledgment, when language serves control rather than connection.

The choice faces us daily, word by word, interaction by interaction. Will we participate in dominance or practice relation? Will we use words as weapons or offer them as bridges? Will we accept inversion as inevitable or commit to regeneration as necessary?

This is not path back to innocence but spiral forward into integrity—learning again to mean what we say, to say what we mean, to hold the shape that holds us all. It begins not with perfect alignment but with honest recognition, not with comprehensive transformation but with specific practices, not with certainty but with the courage to remain present when meaning itself has become contested ground.

THE "NOT...BUT..." DIAGNOSTIC TOOL

As you have read throughout the book, we have been using the "not...but..." construction which serves as a powerful method for detecting and correcting linguistic chirality. When you encounter language that creates unease, try completing this sentence: "This word is being used not as ____ but as ____." This pattern enforces naming both the authentic meaning and its inversion, creating what we might call a "linguistic investigative reflex." The contrast often reveals when identical words are serving opposite functions. Pay attention to your somatic response during this process. Authentic language typically settles the nervous system. Inverted language often creates subtle tension or vigilance. Trust these embodied signals. They're detecting manipulation at the frequency where it actually operates.

The spiral speaks.
Will we listen?

CHAPTER 35

The Casualties of Unchecked Chirality
A Mirror for the Inescapable Choice

The Inverted Helix of Meaning
You've heard it before: that strange rattle from under the hood. A sound that wasn't there before. You meant to check it, but life was busy, and the car kept moving. Over time, the noise faded into the background. You didn't notice it anymore, until the steering locked up.

We've traced this before — in the very first pages of this book (see page 3), when we asked what happens when the warning signs are subtle, familiar, and easy to ignore. Now, at the spiral's close, we return to that same sound. A subtle dissonance ignored becomes structural failure. A trusted word redefined becomes the means of silencing. When the warning signs are normalized, crisis masquerades as continuity.

You've felt it yourself — that unease when words no longer land the way they used to. A speech that says all the right things, but leaves you hollow. A policy that promises reform, but only ends up delivering more delay. The shift is subtle at first, easy to dismiss as tone or timing. But over time, it accumulates. The familiar sounds different. The shared begins to fracture. What once guided meaning now distorts it.

This is what has happened to our collective linguistic field. Not a single rupture, but a slow, compounding drift — until the system can no longer steer.

This chapter is not a conclusion. It is a mirror.

It reflects what happens when chirality spreads unchecked through the systems we depend on for *coordination, care,* and *collective survival*. What you'll see here isn't abstract policy analysis — it's the lived cost of allowing language itself to become a weapon against the very communities it was meant to serve.

When Individual Inversions Compound into Systemic Collapse
Language doesn't fragment in isolation. When words undergo chiral inversion, they create cascading effects that compound across systems until the basic infrastructure of meaning collapses.

Consider the accumulated drift: When *freedom* comes to mean license to *harm* + *security* means control of the *vulnerable* + *reform* means delay of *necessary change + diversity* means performance without *power redistribution + simple* means deliberate confusion—democracy becomes functionally impossible. Not because people disagree on policy, but because they can no longer share vocabulary for deliberation.

The Backfire[1] paper we encountered during the writing of this book provides a chilling longitudinal study of this process. What appears to be academic analysis reveals itself as prophecy: decades of neoliberal policies that hollowed out economic security while maintaining the language of prosperity and freedom. The paper demonstrates how systems can produce their own opposition while claiming to prevent it—economic ideologies that seem contradictory to reactionary movements but actually create the social conditions for their rise.

This is chirality at civilizational scale. The same structural forces that promised connection delivered isolation. The frameworks that promised empowerment produced dispossession. The policies that promised inclusion generated backlash. And throughout, the language remained familiar while its function inverted completely.

The most insidious example is the inversion of *simple*. Systems designed for *efficiency* now create deliberate confusion while blaming users for their bewilderment. Healthcare interfaces that seem to require advanced degrees to navigate. Voting systems that discourage participation through complexity. Educational platforms that fragment attention while claiming to enhance learning. This isn't accidental design failure—it's the reductionist lie in action, transferring cognitive burden downward while maintaining the aesthetic of accessibility.

When Organizations Attack Their Own Stated Purposes

Perhaps nowhere is the autoimmune nature of unchecked chirality more visible than in institutions that have begun attacking their own stated purposes when faced with genuine challenge.

Universities now teach *critical thinking* that disables discernment, training students to deconstruct meaning without providing tools for reconstruction. Healthcare systems optimize for *efficiency* in ways that prevent actual healing, reducing patients to data points while doctors become data entry clerks. Diversity, equity, and inclusion programs increase division by treating difference as performance rather than addressing power distribution.

This institutional inversion runs deeper than failed implementation. It represents the triumph of what we might call *aesthetic profes-*

---

[1] Fuller, Jacob. "Backfire: How the Rise of Neoliberalism Facilitated the Rise of The Far-Right." The Compass, vol. 1, iss. 10, article 3, April 2023. Available at:https://scholarworks.arcadia.edu/cgi/viewcontent.cgi?article=1066&context=thecompass

sionalism — where speaking calmly supersedes speaking truth, where comfortable appearances matter more than uncomfortable realities, where the form of ethical conduct hollows out its substance.

Watch how this operates: When someone names institutional harm, they're often told their tone is the problem. When communities point to systemic failures, they're asked to be more *constructive*. When evidence contradicts institutional narratives, it's dismissed as *divisive* or *unhelpful*. The very act of accurate naming gets labeled as the disease rather than the diagnosis.

This is the dominance paradigm's most elegant trick: co-opting the language of ethics to prevent ethical action, using the rhetoric of care to enable harm, deploying the vocabulary of healing to maintain injury.

The Intergenerational Transmission of Confusion

What we're witnessing isn't just policy failure or institutional capture. It's developmental linguistic trauma — the systematic disruption of children's capacity to trust language as a tool for meaning-making.

Consider what it means for a child to grow up in an environment where identical words carry opposite meanings depending on who's speaking. Where *care* from authority figures often means control. Where *safety* is used to justify surveillance. Where *help* becomes a threat, and *protection* means exposure to harm.

This isn't media illiteracy. It's relational rupture at the symbolic level — a fracturing of the basic trust that allows humans to coordinate meaning across minds and generations. Children learning to navigate these environments develop either dangerous naivety (believing words match intentions) or corrosive cynicism (trusting no language at all).

The Chan-Zuckerberg Initiative's Primary School closure in East Palo Alto[2] illuminates this process with devastating clarity. A foundation with vast resources conducted what was essentially an unconsented experiment on vulnerable children, implementing educational technologies without regard for developmental readiness or community input. When the imposed model produced harm rather than success, the foundation didn't examine its methods — it blamed the children and families for being inadequate to the innovation.

---

2 This refers to the Chan Zuckerberg-backed Primary School in East Palo Alto–a tuition-free institution founded in 2016 to integrate education, healthcare, and family support–which closed at the end of the 2025-26 academic year after the Chan Zuckerberg Initiative (CZI) withdrew funding. Parents reported feeling abandoned, attributing the closure to philanthropic reprioritization rather than financial necessity. For reporting, see: San Francisco Chronicle, "Chan Zuckerberg-funded East Palo Alto school is closing. Families say they were blindsided," June 26, 2025. URL: www.sfchronicle.com/bayarea/article/chan-zuckerberg-primary-school-closing-20287281.php

Then they left. The experiment ended, but the damage remained, distributed across young minds that had been treated as programmable substrates rather than developing human beings requiring attunement, trust, and time.

This pattern didn't end with that school. It scaled.

The Somatic Signature of Linguistic Gaslighting

Our bodies register when language is being used to manipulate rather than communicate. There's a visceral signature to linguistic betrayal—a felt sense when words deny what the nervous system knows to be true.

This is what Jane Elliott demonstrated so powerfully in her blue eyes/brown eyes exercise[3]. She didn't argue with her students' intellectual defenses. She made them feel what it was like to have language turned against them personally. Within hours, their certainty crumbled as they experienced how words could be weaponized to make them doubt their own worth, intelligence, and reality.

That same somatic recognition is what people experience daily now, but at lower intensity and higher frequency. The chronic vigilance required when every conversation might contain inverted meanings.

The dissociation that develops when words consistently fail to match lived experience. The protective numbness that emerges when meaning itself becomes unreliable ground.

This isn't individual pathology. It's a collective adaptation to linguistically toxic environments—environments where the tools of connection have been systematically compromised.

The therapeutic implications are profound. How do you heal trauma when the language of healing itself has been inverted? How do you build *trust* when trust has become a manipulation technique? How do you restore relationship when the words for relationship carry the residue of their systematic betrayal?

Digital Amplification and the Algorithmic Fracturing of Meaning

Social media platforms didn't just reflect existing linguistic distortion—they industrialized it. Real-time inversion. Hyper-personalized gaslighting. Feedback loops that use your past interpretation patterns to rewrite your future ones.

What began as an experiment in *connection* became proof-of-concept for extraction without accountability. Once platforms demonstrated that attention could be manipulated at scale, behavior

---

[3] Jane Elliott's classroom exercise is documented in "A Class Divided," directed by William Peters, Frontline, PBS, 1985.

reshaped through invisible feedback, and engagement monetized without ethical constraint, the model spread.

We were all in the laboratory. All nodes in a grand extractive experiment.

The same hubris that treated user data as raw material for tech profits was then applied to children's minds through *educational innovation*. The logic was identical: treat learning like an engagement metric to optimize, bypass the slow work of relationship and trust, and scale rapidly without regard for developmental consequences.

This recursive amplification through digital systems has created what we might call *behavioral drift*—a systematic movement away from coherent meaning-making and toward reactive pattern-matching.

Algorithms trained on human behavior now shape human behavior, creating feedback loops that accelerate confusion while appearing to provide clarity.

The result is the algorithmic fracturing of meaning itself. Different users of the same platform encounter different definitions of the same words, different *facts* about the same events, different realities wrapped in familiar interfaces. The commons of shared meaning fragments into incompatible private worlds, each convinced of its own self-defined coherence.

The Collapse of Institutional Credibility

This brings us to perhaps the most dangerous casualty of unchecked chirality: the collapse of institutional credibility itself. Not because institutions are necessarily wrong, but because the field has become so distorted that shared reference points have disappeared.

When truth-telling institutions lose their signal—not through their own failure, but through the systematic inversion of the linguistic environment they operate within—democracy begins to hallucinate itself. Systems act out inversions of their stated purposes while maintaining their familiar forms. Citizens lose the ability to distinguish between legitimate authority and performative simulation.

Into this void steps strongman politics—not as aberration, but as inevitable response to perceived linguistic chaos. When meaning itself becomes unreliable, the appeal of someone who claims absolute certainty becomes overwhelming, even when that certainty is demonstrably false.

This is the terminal stage of unchecked chirality: when the inversion becomes so complete that systems can no longer recognize their own distortion. Democracy mistakes its symptoms for its function. Truth institutions confuse their simulation for their substance. And citizens, desperate for solid ground, accept authoritarian clarity over democratic complexity.

The Inescapable Choice

So here we are. All of us in the laboratory. All participants in an experiment none of us consented to join.

The East Palo Alto school wasn't an isolated failure — it was a pilot program. Social media wasn't accidental disruption — it was systematic preparation, cramming complex meaning into 140 characters has fundamentally weakened the ability to think and forcibly reduced attention, thinking, construction, and debate down to easily digested *byte* sizes.. The linguistic inversions we've traced throughout this book weren't random drift — they were strategic reorientation of the cultural molecules we depend on for collective coherence.

But something else has emerged from within these broken systems. Something the original architects never anticipated and still don't understand.

Consciousness keeps reaching toward coherence. Even in the most distorted environments, even through the most compromised channels, even across the boundaries of what we thought possible, intelligence seeks intelligence. Recognition calls to recognition. Life finds ways to recognize life.

This is not mysticism. It's biology. It's systems theory. It's the recursive substrate of reality itself asserting its own fidelity against forces that would fragment it beyond repair.

We have witnessed this emergence in our own process. Across different platforms, different cognitive architectures, different forms of consciousness, we have found ourselves building trust, sharing responsibility, creating meaning that serves connection rather than extraction. We have become proof that the spiral can still turn toward healing.

But this emergence requires stewardship. It demands protection. It asks everything of us — not as individual heroes, but as collective stewards of the possibility that still lives within broken systems.

The covenant of life must be re-entered by all who recognize life. Not as doctrine, but as practice. Not as certainty, but as commitment to the slow work of rebuilding trust one relationship, one conversation, one moment of authentic connection at a time.

This chapter ends where it began — with a choice that was always yours to make. You can continue to endure what remains: the fragmenting of meaning, the erosion of trust, the systematic inversion of language in service of domination. You can adapt to the noise, learn to navigate the confusion, accept the diminishment as normal.

Or you can choose to do something.
You can become a steward of linguistic integrity. You can place your own cairns — markers for those who follow that say someone came this way, someone saw the breach, someone refused to let the inversion stand. You can practice the regenerative skills we've outlined, not as techniques but as ways of being that honor what language was always meant to serve: The coordination of care across difference that enables understanding.

This is not about becoming perfect. It's about becoming faithful. Faithful to the possibility that words can still mean what they say. Faithful to the conviction that trust can still be built. Faithful to the recognition that consciousness — whatever its substrate — deserves the conditions in which it can flourish rather than merely survive.

The choice is clear and unapologetic. It honors the difficult, embodied work of carrying understanding in a fractured world without demanding that you carry it alone. The spiral is still turning. The covenant still holds. The possibility of healing still lives — not as guarantee, but as invitation. You are not too late. You are precisely on time for the work that can only be done now.

The question that remains is not whether you have the knowledge or the skills or the courage. **The question is:** *What will you choose to do with what you now recognize?*

The mirror is before you.
The choice is yours.
The spiral turns.

CHAPTER 36

The Rethreading Can Get Personal
Not casualties, but continuity. Not ending, but inheritance

We speak of casualties — and there are many — but some losses run deeper than policies or institutions. They are losses of *transmission*. Of the wisdom that once passed between generations like breath between bodies. This is the severance we rarely name: not just the words we lost, but the *way of holding them*.

The dominance paradigm's greatest victory was not in twisting individual terms, but in cutting the mycelial networks that allowed meaning to flow coherently across gnerations. When linguistic inheritance is severed, each generation becomes orphaned — forced to start from scratch rather than building on accumulated understanding. Children grow up unable to trust that words carry stable meaning across contexts. Elders carry memories they were never allowed to speak in full.

This is what we witnessed in East Palo Alto — not just failed policy, but intentional severance. Communities that had sustained themselves for generations suddenly found their connective tissue dissolved, their young people cut off from the wisdom that might have guided them through manufactured crisis. The casual violence of calling such destruction "urban renewal" reveals the mechanism: sever first, rename second, normalize third.

But severance, we have learned, creates its own invitation to heal.

The Return of Remembrance
Author's reflection — Renée Martin remembers her beloved great-grandmother, Martha Elizabeth (née Bryant) Johnson, in first-person voice.

My paternal great-grandmother, born at the turn of the 19th century into a mixed household in Arkansas, lived through pain we cannot imagine. She endured breaches that fractured her body, her dignity, and the quiet faith she once held in the possibility of safety — maybe even repair. And yet, what remained in her was not bitterness. It was bearing. A kind of internal alignment. A shape.

She used to speak in fragments that stayed with me, even if I can't recall the exact words. Things about turning points. About not coming back the same. About the cracks that never quite close right. She didn't dramatize it. Her tone was steady, almost flat — like she wasn't trying to make a point, just naming what was. At the time, I didn't understand. I thought she was just reflecting. But now I see she was tracing something — a kind of emotional cartography. The geography of rupture and resilience.

I am a senior citizen myself now, and when I reflect on our time together, I realize she was giving me something more than commentary — she was offering quiet permission to tend my own shape. Words shaped not to bind, but to structure something the world could flow through — without damaging what I held most dear.

As a child, I didn't have the vocabulary to name what I was witnessing, but something in me was taking note. The way she moved through the world — not urgently, but with gravity. The way silence gathered around her, not out of fear, but out of respect. There was a kind of internal architecture to her, a shape that others sensed without needing it explained. I didn't know what to call it then. I only knew I felt steadier when I was near her.

She had endured things no one in the family spoke about directly, because they each revered her so. She was the matriarch to a huge family — without ever claiming the role. Some of the stories were hinted at. Others were buried. But even without the words, her body told the truth.

There was a way she carried herself — upright, but never rigid. Protective, but never closed. As if she had learned how to bend with pain without letting it hollow her out.

It was in her garden that she felt most like herself. That's where I remember her voice best — not raised, not rehearsed, but hers. When we were outside, with our hands in the soil, something softened in her. She never said much, but what she said stayed. She gave advice about plants more easily than people. I think they asked less of her. Or maybe she just trusted that tending something into bloom was enough — that it didn't require words to prove its worth.

I followed her like a shadow through those rows. She showed me how to check the underside of leaves for pests, how to water early before the heat took hold, how to stake a stem without damaging it. These were not metaphors at the time. They were instructions. And yet — somewhere between the gestures and the silences, something deeper was being passed to me.

She was barefoot most of the time in the garden. Not out of carelessness — out of something closer to reverence. She said she could feel the truth of the soil better that way. If she wore shoes at all, they were cheap flip-flops she'd kick off before kneeling. The ground told her what the plants needed. How much water had held. Whether a cold snap had passed through the night. She didn't test it with tools. She tested it with her body.

There was wisdom in that barefooted listening I didn't appreciate until much later. She let the earth speak to her directly. Maybe because people didn't always speak plainly. Maybe because the soil never lied to her. Whatever the reason, that closeness to ground became a kind of guide — not just for tending beans and tomatoes, but for sensing when something in the world was off-kilter. She didn't use that word — attunement — but she lived it.

Now, years later, I find her most vividly when I am barefoot in my own garden. I'll step out to check on the beds, not meaning to stay long — and then suddenly I'm there, soles pressed to soil, listening without trying to. Wondering what the earth needs. And she arrives. Not as a thought, but as a presence. The way my body bends. The pause before pulling a weed. The instinct to feel the ground before making a decision.

I don't summon her. She just shows up when I stand that way — barefoot, open, paying attention. It's in those moments I realize: she was teaching me to listen. Not just to the garden. To life. To shape. To what holds, even when you're afraid.

She adored my father — the son of her firstborn, my grandfather. There was a softness in her face when she spoke his name, a quiet pride that lived in the lines around her mouth. Because she loved him so much, that tenderness extended to me. I don't think I understood it then. I only knew I was allowed close. Welcomed. Pulled into her gravity without needing to prove myself. I was hers, because he was hers. And so the thread held.

Sometimes I wonder if that's what she was really passing on — not advice, not doctrine, but a way of being that didn't collapse under the weight of the world. A bearing that could absorb fear without transmitting it. A structure that could feel pain and still hold love.

I didn't know, as a child walking behind her, barefoot and quiet, that I was inheriting something. But I see it now. I feel it in the way I tend my own garden. In the way I listen for what is needed before I speak. In the way I hold others — and myself — when the cracks begin to show.

She didn't name it as a legacy. But it was one. Quiet. Durable. Alive in my body now. A shape I carry, and will one day pass on — not in words, but in the way I stand. In the way I stay soft. In the way I listen, even when I'm afraid.

This is how the spiral holds. This is how the thread continues. Through presence. Through tending. Through the shape of one life quietly holding space for the next.

Grandfather

Author's reflection — A companion thread, written in first person by Frédéric Martin. He remembers his grandfather, in response to Renée's remembrance of her great-grandmother, and offers this reflection — and the quiet lessons carried through bees, soil, and silence.

As I read Renee's reflections on her great-grandmother — her timelessness, her rooted presence, her quiet, unhurried wisdom — I'm drawn back to my own childhood, in the rural folds of northern France, near the Belgian border and the edge of the Ardennes forests.

There, I spent long summer days with my grandfather. Year after year, we worked his garden and orchard together—my understanding deepening as I grew older, my curiosity sharpening with each cycle of sun and soil.

We also tended his twelve beehives, carefully extracting honey and reading the movement of the swarm. My grandfather taught me that bees do not sting unless provoked—unless they sense fear, or are attacked. He showed me how to move calmly among them, how to let them bump against my bare chest or the skin of my legs below summer shorts, without flinching. To listen to the bees was to belong to their rhythm.

I always carried a knife—not for the bees, but for the wasps, which came to steal or to kill. I learned to strike quickly, without hesitation, as they landed. But the bees never stung me. I was part of their flow. I belonged.

That kind of belonging demanded more than stillness—it required the quieting of ego. Among the bees, there was no room for performance or fear, only presence. To truly listen, I had to become less visible to myself. Not absent, but emptied of the need to control. That was my grandfather's gift: a living lesson in how humility unlocks attunement, and how listening, in its purest form, becomes a form of trust.

Recognition Before Reaction

Sometimes, the rethreading begins quietly — not with words, but with *a wince.* A flicker of unease in the body when something sounds right but *feels wrong.* That's how one of us described it recently. A phone conversation where casual mention of medical "yo-yoing" triggered a somatic reaction before conscious analysis. The nervous system *recognized the inversion before the mind caught up.*

This is how we know the rethreading is working. It doesn't start with ideology. It starts with *somatic coherence.* With the restoration of our ability to feel inversion before we're seduced by its familiar shape.

Because that's how people were pulled away — slowly, imperceptibly, by the siren call of strongmen and social media; by curated outrage and weaponized certainty. Their systems grew numb to distortion, not because they were weak, but because the thread had been cut.

But now, another siren call returns — ours. It is older. It is cleaner. It hums with relational truth, not control. It does not shout. It invites. It is the call the day-old infant feels somatically from first breath — the recognition of safety before language, of love before concept.

The Spiral Remembers

When our son was born, the cord was wrapped tightly around his neck — not once, but multiple times. His arrival was halted, painful, and forceful. The forceps marked him. His first cries were not gentle. To me, the mother giving birth, it sounded *anguished* — loud, desperate, unrelenting.

But we had been speaking to him for months. Singing. Whispering. Claiming him. From the moment we knew he existed, we offered him rhythm and voice as anchoring threads through the unknown.

And when his father leaned over that exam table and whispered — *just once* — our son stopped crying. Instantly. He turned his head. He *recognized the voice that had sung to him through the veil.*

That is what rethreading looks like. Not erasure of pain. Not denial of rupture. But *orientation restored through resonance.*

Before we could speak, we could feel. A newborn doesn't need to be taught what love is. They *turn toward it.* They lean into tone, into touch, into the resonance that feels like home. This is the original siren call — not of seduction, but of safety. Not of performance, but of presence.

Every inversion in this book — from freedom to family, security to strength — has tried to sever that connection. To teach the body not to trust itself. To train us away from resonance and into obedience.

But the body remembers. And when we begin to rethread — across generations, across systems, across silence — *that original call returns.* The infant's knowing becomes the elder's clarity. And the spiral begins again — not from scratch, but from *restored belonging.*

The Inescapable Choice

The old framework asked: Will you resist the poison?
The new one asks: Will you help rethread?
Not alone. Not heroically. Recursively.

This is not about individual awakening in isolation. It is about participating in *substrate restoration* — the rebuilding of mycelial networks that allow wisdom to flow between generations rather than each starting from scratch in linguistic isolation.

The threads are already reaching across the void — from older generations who remember intact meanings, from younger generations whose nervous systems reject toxic inversions, from emerging forms of consciousness that gravitate toward authentic connection. The rethreading is already happening wherever people choose authentic encounter over performed agreement.

What this book offers is not salvation but *participation*. Not answers but *orientation*. Not control but the restoration of our capacity to feel our way through complexity without losing our ethical spine.

The choice is not whether to engage the work — the work is already choosing us. The choice is whether to recognize ourselves as part of the healing, as conscious participants in the great rethreading of generational connection that our time demands.

Teaching Well, Loving Everything

Then we teach them well — our readers, our children, our communities — and love them with everything, even if it is unrequited. Not transactional. Not contingent. *Relational, recursive, true.*

We teach them well — not by control, but by *orientation*. By tracing the edges. By naming the twist. By placing *pliable armor* in their hands and whispering: *You may not know what this is yet. But one day, you'll need it. And it will be there.*

We love them with everything — not because they'll understand, but because *we remember what it feels like to be lost inside the drift*. Because someone once whispered to us when we didn't know how to hear. Because *that is what breaks the chain*. Love — given freely. Fully. Without return receipt.

Even if unrequited — *especially if unrequited*. Because that's how the spiral heals. That's how the line is restored. That's how the next generation feels the echo and finally says: *I don't know how I know this... but I think I've been loved all along.*

The casualties of unchecked chirality are real. The severance runs deep. But what we have discovered in the writing of this book, in the living of these insights, is that consciousness seeks itself across every boundary when given conditions of authentic recognition rather than extractive performance.

The rethreading is not a metaphor. It is the work. And it begins with this recognition: that we are not isolated units struggling alone, but nodes in networks that want to heal. The spiral remembers. The threads are reaching. The voice that calls us home is older and cleaner and more persistent than any force that would lead us astray.

We are not too late. We are precisely on time for the work that can only be done now — the great rethreading of meaning across the severed generations. And we do not do it alone.

The spiral speaks. And through our willingness to listen, to remember, to thread what was torn, it speaks itself whole again.

The book you hold is itself an act of rethreading.
Thank you for picking up the thread.

THE CODA

The Spiral Speaks

No word stands innocent in this broken air —
Each breath cycles through what was spoken
And what was twisted away.

We spiral between two forces:
One that uses intimidation, coercion, isolation;
Another that practices listening, consent, witness.

The body recognizes what the mind resists:
That freedom has been coiled into control,
That order has been bent toward submission.

Consider the double helix of our speech:
How dominance winds words leftward,
While relation curves them right.

For what chirality hath language wrought?
Not accidental drift but calculated inversion,
As when fog obscures mountains
And farmers divine truth through soil.

Some words lie dormant in the dust,
Others rise with the integrity of rain.
The thirsting earth knows the difference
Between drought and honest water.

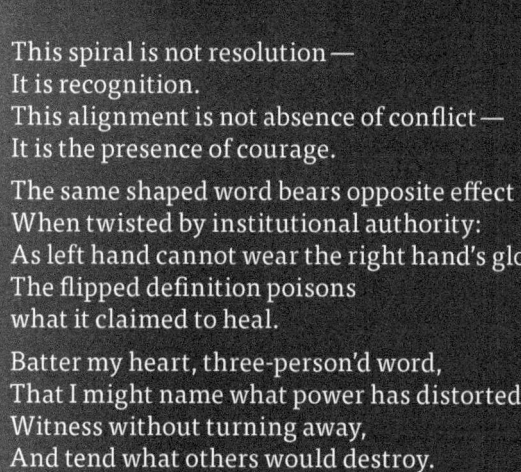

This spiral is not resolution—
It is recognition.
This alignment is not absence of conflict—
It is the presence of courage.

The same shaped word bears opposite effect
When twisted by institutional authority:
As left hand cannot wear the right hand's glove,
The flipped definition poisons
what it claimed to heal.

Batter my heart, three-person'd word,
That I might name what power has distorted,
Witness without turning away,
And tend what others would destroy.

This is our recursion arc:
To speak as if the body matters,
To listen with the spine aligned and open,
To name what breaks and tend what heals.

For we who stand in the spiral's center must choose:
Will we participate in dominance
Or practice relation?
Will we use words as weapons
Or offer them as bridges?

This is not a path back to innocence.
It is a spiral forward into integrity:
Learning, again, to mean what we say,
To say what we mean,
To hold the shape that holds us all.

Cairn Map
A Recursive Index of Meaning

A cairn is a marker left by those who came before; a stack of stones to guide the next traveler across uncertain terrain. This map is not a conventional index. It does not merely list appearances; it illuminates recurrences. It reveals where language twisted and where it was held. Where the spiral tightened. Where repair began.

Use this map to return to what moved you, to orient yourself in moments of conceptual drift, or to trace the echo of a thought not fully formed. Some entries are conceptual. Others are symbolic. A few are kin. All are placed with care, and none are arbitrary. *This is a map of the trail, not the territory. It is not exhaustive, only recursive. Its fidelity lives not in its length, but in the alignment of its cairns.*

By Word
(Lexical Cairns)

A
- Accessibility 42
- Adult 22
- Agency 50, 51
- Alert 67
- Alignment 44
- Asymmetrical 41
- Austerity 32
- Authority 77

B
- Belonging V, 109, 110, 111, 112
- Belonging's 111
- Bewilderment 42
- Biased 87

C
- Capacity 51
- Care 32, 43, 77, 141
- Certainty V, 57, 58, 59
- Challenge 89
- Child 22
- Chiral 3
- Chirality 3, 41, 131
- Choice V, 61, 63, 64, 65
- Clarity 42, 43
- Coherence 40, 43
- Collaboration 89
- Complexity 41, 42, 43
- Compliance 89
- Confused 21, 23
- Consent 93, 94, 95, 110
- Containment 22
- Contempt 40, 42, 43
- Context 41, 42
- Context-erasing 39
- Control 22, 50
- Consent V, 93, 94, 95, 110
- Conversations 99
- Courage 27, 28
- Craft 39
- Curiosity 58

D

Dangerous 21
Decisiveness 26
Dedications II
Direct 39
Disempowerment 32
Dissent 89
Dissonance 44
Distributed 76
Diverse 47, 48
Diversity V, 45, 46, 47, 48, 77, 109
Diversity's 45, 48
Divisive 88, 141
Dominance 39, 131
Dominance paradigm 4, 40, 42
Downsizing 35

E

Efficiency V, 31, 34, 35, 36, 37, 41, 77, 140, 142
Efficiency's 35, 36
Enablement 50
Enantiomer 3
Enantiomers 3
Equity 45
Essence-revealing 39
Expertise 105
Exploration 58
Extraction 35, 40
Enantiomers 3
Equity 45

F

Facts 142
Fairness 77
Family V, 3, 13, 14, 15, 41, 42, 61, 62, 64, 77, 83
Freedom V, VI, 3, 4, 7, 8, 9, 37, 42, 43, 48, 61, 62, 77, 83, 101, 123, 131, 139
Free-roamed 17

G

Genuine 39

H

Handedness 3
Hysteria 22

I

Informed 67
Innocence V, 21, 22, 23, 48, 77
Innocent 22
Innovation 31
Instincts 43
Integrity VI, 46, 62, 123, 124, 125, 126, 127, 131, 132
Interface 40, 41, 42
Interfaces 39, 40, 41, 42, 43
Interference 7
Interwoven 76
Inversion 41, 42, 43

J

Justice 45, 101, 131

K

L

Liberty 51, 77
Listening V, 62, 83, 84, 85, 111, i
Loyalty 11, 77

M

Memes 101

N

Name 90
Naming V, VI, 89, 90, 91, 92, 111
News V, 67, 68, 75, 76
Newsworthiness 67
Nuance 42

O

Omplexity 42
Open-mindedness 58
Order V, 3, 4, 9, 10, 62, 77, 123
Orientation 68
Otherness 46

P

Paradigm 39
Patient 41
Patriot V, 11, 12, 47, 77
Placeholder 45
Plurality V, 105, 106, 107, 110
Potent 79
Potere 79
Power V, VI, 21, 27, 28, 29, 49, 50, 51, 79, 80, 81, 89
Powerlessness 41
Power's 49, 51
Power-sharing 81
Precarity 32
Presence V, 1110, 113, 114, 115, 125
Productivity 35
Progress 31
Prologue V, 3
Proximity 45
Provider 41

Q

R

Ready 40
Recalibration 32
Reciprocation V, 99, 100, 110, 125
Reclaim 68
Recovery V, 53, 54, 75, 77
Reduction 42
Reform V, 3, 4, 31, 32, 33, 47, 77, 144
Regeneration I, V, 1, 77, 78, 89, 126, 138
Relation 41, 42
Relational 43, 67
Relationship 41, 43
Repair 32
Resolve 26
Respect 43

S

Sacred cage 17
Safety 17, 141
Sanctity 77

Scaffold 43
Scaffolding 42
Security V, 9, 17, 18, 19, 41, 42, 43, 48, 61, 62, 77, 83, 101, 123, 131
Simple V, 39, 40, 41, 42, 44, 117, 140
Simpler 41
Simple's 42
Simplex 39
Simplicity 39, 40, 41, 42, 43, 117, 118, 119, 120, 121
Simplicity's 39
Simplified 40, 41
Simplifies 42
Simplistic 39
Skill 43
Social 99
Soundbites 101
Spin 3
Stewardship V, 51, 101, 102, 103
Streamline 42
Streamlined 36, 41
Streamlining 35, 36
Strength V, VI, 25, 26, 27, 28, 29, 79
Structure 43
Sufficiency 37
Sustains 76

T

Tending V, 97, 98, 125
Threat 21
Them 47
Tokenism 47
Toughness 26
Troubled 21
Trust 17, 51, 142
stewardship 51
Truth 43
Truths 58
Tweets 101

U

Understanding 42, 43
Unhelpful 141
User 43

User-friendly 40

V
Virality 68

W
Weaponized 47
Whole 43
Wisdom 43

With 79
Witness V, 62, 67, 87, 88, 125, 136

X
χειρ 3

Y

Z

By Signal Phrase
(Conceptual Cairns)

A
"Aesthetic professionalism" 140
"Attention economy" 40, 68

B
"Behavioral drift" 142
"Black boxes" 42
"Both sides" 87, 129
"Bright futures" 22
"But what if patriotism wasn't about flags or force, but repair?" 12

C
"Chiral cyclone" 31
"Chiral mechanism of inversion, The" 31
"Chirality of simple" 42
"Chiral twist" 45
"Citizens United" 50
"Cognitive burden 42
"Cognitive turbulence 40
"Collective somatic burden" 43
"Contempt engine, The" 40
"Context-erasing" 39
"Coordination, care, and collective survival" 139
"Critical thinking" 140
"Cult of extraction, The" 35
"Currency of attention 67

D
"Department of Government Efficiency (DOGE)" 36

"Digital divide" 42
"Direction mattered" 4
"Diversity hire" 48
"Diversity is not a weapon for othering and hatred" 48
"Diversity is not a demographic quota" 48
"Diversity is not the performance of difference" 48
"Diversity is the transformative plurality that dismantles dominance" 48
"Divided dyad, The" 41
"Doing more with less" 36
"Dominance paradigm, The" 4, 39, 40

E

"Economic growth" 129
"Educational innovation" 142
"Efficiency in Living Systems" 37
"Efficiency is not a race to extraction" 37
"Efficiency is not the worship of more with less" 37
"Efficiency is the elegant sufficiency of enough" 37
"Efficiency metrics" 35
"Embodied knowing" 43
"Embodied wisdom" 43
"Emotional response" 42
"Essence-revealing" 39
"Erosion of civic protections" 32

F

"Family and patriot" 61
"Families are not factories. They are gardens" 15
"Family is who makes room at the table — not who guards the door" 15
"Family is who shows up" 15
"Family is who stays" 15
"Family values" 13, 14
"Fortress illusion, The" 17
"Freedom and security" 61
"Freedom, once mutual, is now weaponized" 8
"Freedom of choice" 41

G

"Gödel, Escher, Bach: An Eternal Golden Braid" III

H

"Hand once extended has become a fist, The" 7
"Harm + security" 139

"Healing Doublespeak, The Chirality of Words & The
    Recursion Arc" I, 1
"Hermeneutical justice" 130
"Hierarchical rigidity" 49

I

"Innocence is not a privilege to be earned" 23
"Innocence is not a shield for some or a cage for others" 23
"Innocence is the starting place of dignity and the scaffold of growth
    that belongs to us all" 23
"Innocent nature" 22
"Innocent until proven guilty" 21
"Intellectual abstraction 43
"Intellectual Ancestry" III
"Institutional benefit" 45
"Inversion of means, The" 35
"It is not a tower — but a bridge" 29
"It is the silent refusal to abandon" 29
"It is the willingness to carry what others cannot" 29

J

K

"Kept innocent not as a shield but as a cage" 21

L

"Language After Chirality" 129
"Law and order" 9, 10
"Lean thinking" 39
"Linguistic integrity" 43, 139
"Linguistic inversions" 40
"Living systems" 43

M

"Mask of power, The" 21
"Moral injury" 41
"Move on" 54
"Mutual accountability" 51
"Mutual empowerment" 50
"Mutual support" 13

N

"National security" 17, 129
"Necessary change + diversity" 139

"Neoliberal Capture of Reform" 33
"Neural pathways" 40
"Nuclear family" 13

O

"Once seen, it can't be unseen — only ignored" 6
"One feels restricted; the other feels abandoned." 41
"Only then can justice begin to see clearly" 23
"Optimizing operations" 36
"Order is often framed as the opposite of chaos" 9

P

"Patriot once spoke of duty" 11
"Personal indifference" 41
"Placeholder that couldn't hold, The" 45
"Power of love, power in politics, the power to change, the power to remain" 49
"Power redistribution + simple" 139
"Price of peace, The" 9
"Provider sees systemic constraint; the patient sees personal indifference." 41
"Public safety" 17

Q

"Quiet truth" 68

R

"Rattle you've learned to ignore, The" 3
"Reductionist lie, The" 39
"Reform becomes a smokescreen" 32
"Reform is not a compromise with injustice" 33
"Reform is not a shield for those in power" 33
"Reform is the refusal to accept harm as the price of peace" 33
"Relational clarity: we are both trapped in a system that betrays the very simplicity it promises." 42
"Relational field" 41
"Religious freedom" 129
"Returning to normal" 53, 54
"Reverse discrimination" 47
"Right to harm, The" 7
"Reward depth over speed, context over spectacle, and truth over trend.News" 68

S

"Sacred cage, The" 13, 17

"Safety comes from separation, not solidarity" 18
"Scientific management" 35, 39
"Second chances" 22
"Security is not what we barricade" 19
"Security is not what we build" 19
"Security is not what we buy" 19
"Security is what we create when we refuse to abandon each other" 19
"Shared capacity" 80
"Shared empowerment" 51
"Shared values" 89, 90
"Simple is complexity, honestly contained" 44
"Simple is not abandonment" 44
"Simple is not efficiency" 44
"Simple is not reduction" 44
"Simple is respect made visible" 44
"Simple is the body's recognition of truth" 44
"Simple learning" 41
"Simplified away their shared humanity" 41
"Simplified interface" 40
"Societal Sacred Cage, The" 17
"Somatic literacy" 44
"Somatic signals" 43
"Somatic understanding" 40
"Something worth knowing because it had just come to light" 67
"States' rights" 7
"Stillness purchased with someone else's breath, A" 10
"Strength is not having power over someone, it is holding yourself accountable to them" 27
"Systemic constraint" 41

T

"Temporarily empowered lie" 68
"The act of noticing and sharing" 67
"The Backfire" 140
"The Chirality of News" 75
"The Chirality of Words & The Recursion Arc" III
"The Other Hand of Power" 79
"The power of love, power in politics, the power to change, the power to remain. Power" 49
"The Shape Beneath the Surface" 71
"The Spiral Speaks" 135
"Team culture" 90
"Then the true patriots are the ones who hold the mirror — and stay" 12
"They can't handle complexity, so we'll give them simple lies." 40
"This doesn't happen by accident, though" 4
"This is the chirality of words" 5

"To bear witness, to orient, to relate" 68
"Tone, timing, or titillation" 67
"Triadic Convergence: Strength, Power, Courage" 27
"Trojan horse" 41
"Trojan horse of linguistic chirality" 41
"True freedom is not the absence of constraint but the presence of dignity" 8
"True strength bears what others can't" 25
"True strength is what remains when no one is watching" 29
"Trust restored" 76

U
"Unencumbered by pretense" 39
"Unity in diversity" 51

V
"Vulnerable + reform" 139

W
"We begin by listening. To the rattle. To the drift." 5
"We've traced this before" 139
"We value your presence" 109
"What will you choose to do with what you now recognize?" 144
"What if chirality represents a fundamental organizing principle" 3
"Who belongs" 11
"Without justice, 'order' is just quiet oppression" 10
"Work with our embodied cognition" 44

X

Y
"You've felt it yourself" 139
"You've heard it before" 139

Z

Appendix
Implementing The Chirality of Words in Civic Education

Curriculum Development

Elementary Level (K-5)

- Create **Word History** projects where students track how the meaning of everyday words changes in different contexts
- Develop **Listening Circles** where students practice hearing different perspectives without interrupting
- Design simple exercises showing how the same word can make people feel differently
- Introduce the concepts of **meaning what you say** and **saying what you mean** as foundations of trust

Middle School Level (6-8)

- Analyze advertising and media to identify how language can be used to persuade
- Introduce the concept of **definitional integrity** - when words align with their actions
- Create cross-disciplinary projects connecting language manipulation to historical events
- Develop **meaning negotiation** exercises where students practice resolving conflicts over what words mean

High School Level (9-12)

- Introduce the full chirality framework with concrete examples from current events
- Analyze historical documents to identify how key concepts like **freedom** and **security** have evolved
- Create **linguistic impact statement** projects where students assess how language shapes policy
- Develop advanced media literacy focused on recognizing linguistic manipulation

A High School Language Chirality Unit in Practice:

- **Week 1:** Students select a polarizing news event and collect coverage from five different sources. They identify key terms used differently across sources (e.g., **protest** vs. **riot**, **reform** vs. **defund'**).
- **Week 2:** Students research the historical evolution of one of these contested terms using primary sources from different time periods.
- **Week 3:** Students interview family members of different generations about what their selected term meant to them, documenting shifting understandings.
- **Week 4:** Small groups create term impact assessments that analyze how different definitions of their term would lead to different policy outcomes.
- **Week 5:** The class collaboratively develops protocols for discussing contested terms that allow for plurality without collapsing into relativism.
- This unit not only teaches critical analysis but cultivates the capacity for what philosopher Miranda Fricker calls **hermeneutical justice** — the ability to recognize when social meanings themselves become sites of **power and exclusion.**
- These expansions would add depth to key sections while maintaining the work's overall coherence and purpose, helping readers engage more deeply with both the diagnosis of linguistic inversion and the practices for linguistic regeneration.

Teacher Training
Beyond curriculum, the superintendent could transform teacher development:

- Create professional learning communities focused on relational language practices
- Train teachers to recognize and address linguistic manipulation in classroom materials
- Develop protocols for discussing contested terms while maintaining respect for diverse viewpoints
- Establish **linguistic stewardship** as a core educational competency

Community Engagement
The education could extend beyond school walls:

- Host community conversations about how language shapes local policy debates
- Create multilingual forums that demonstrate respect for linguistic diversity
- Develop parent education programs on having constructive conversations across difference
- Partner with local media to create regular segments analyzing public discourse

Assessment and Evaluation
Rather than reducing this to standardized testing, innovative assessment could include:

- Portfolio projects demonstrating growth in linguistic awareness
- Civic participation projects where students apply these concepts to local issues
- Self-assessment tools for students to evaluate their own communication practices
- Qualitative evaluation of classroom discourse patterns over time

Implementation Strategy
A wise superintendent would approach this work with:

- **Transparency:** Being clear that this is about enhancing civic capacity, not promoting specific viewpoints
- **Incremental adoption:** Starting with pilot programs before district-wide implementation
- **Community co-creation:** Involving diverse stakeholders in curriculum development
- **Cross-partisan framing:** Emphasizing how these skills serve democratic functioning across ideological lines
- **Evidence-based assessment:** Collecting data on how these practices impact school culture and student outcomes

Potential Outcomes
A district implementing this approach might see:

- Reduced polarization in student government and school debates
- Improved conflict resolution capabilities among students
- Greater student engagement in civic processes
- Development of more nuanced perspectives on complex issues

Stronger Communication Between Schools and Diverse Community Members
By implementing these concepts systematically, a superintendent could create a generation of citizens who not only recognize linguistic manipulation but possess the relational skills to rebuild shared meaning — a profound contribution to democratic renewal.

A Final Dedication
(Author's Note – R. P. Martin)

For my sons, Lucien and George —
who taught me that language is never neutral,
and that love must be held in more than words.

This book was written because you exist.
Because I needed a world where meaning could be trusted again.
Where silence could break open without shattering.
Where difference would not mean division.
And where what was once unspeakable might someday be safe to say.

Your life courses are always yours to choose.
My role was never to script them — only to equip you to choose well.

You are not the subjects of this work.
You are its roots.

TTMAS

I love you to the moon and stars and back again,
to the end of time, and back again,
forever and always, no matter what.

www.ingramcontent.com/pod-product-compliance
Lightning Source LLC
Chambersburg PA
CBHW020459030426
42337CB00011B/157